Intelligence and Human Progress

Intelligence and Human Progress
The Story of What was Hidden in our Genes

James R. Flynn

ELSEVIER

AMSTERDAM • BOSTON • HEIDELBERG • LONDON
NEW YORK • OXFORD • PARIS • SAN DIEGO
SAN FRANCISCO • SINGAPORE • SYDNEY • TOKYO
Academic Press is an imprint of Elsevier

Academic Press is an imprint of Elsevier
The Boulevard, Langford Lane, Kidlington, Oxford, OX5 1GB, UK
225 Wyman Street, Waltham, MA 02451, USA

First published 2013

Notices
Knowledge and best practice in this field are constantly changing. As new research and
experience broaden our understanding, changes in research methods, professional practices, or
medical treatment may become necessary.

Practitioners and researchers must always rely on their own experience and knowledge
in evaluating and using any information, methods, compounds, or experiments described herein.
In using such information or methods they should be mindful of their own safety and the safety
of others, including parties for whom they have a professional responsibility.

To the fullest extent of the law, neither the Publisher nor the authors, contributors, or editors,
assume any liability for any injury and/or damage to persons or property as a matter of products
liability, negligence or otherwise, or from any use or operation of any methods, products,
instructions, or ideas contained in the material herein.

British Library Cataloguing in Publication Data
A catalogue record for this book is available from the British Library

Library of Congress Cataloging-in-Publication Data
A catalog record for this book is available from the Library of Congress

ISBN: 978-0-12-417014-8

For information on all Academic Press publications
visit our website at **store.elsevier.com**

This book has been manufactured using Print On Demand technology. Each copy is produced
to order and is limited to black ink. The online version of this book will show color figures
where appropriate.

Working together
to grow libraries in
developing countries

ELSEVIER | **Book Aid International**

www.elsevier.com • www.bookaid.org

Transferred to Digital Printing in 2013

DEDICATION

To Steven Pinker

Who did so much to fortify my resolve

For the Colonel's Lady and Judy O'Grady are sisters under their skins.

Kipling (1896)

CONTENTS

LIST OF TABLES AND FIGURE

Tables

Figure

ACKNOWLEDGMENTS

Steven Pinker, to whom this book is dedicated, is of course not responsible for any of its flaws. Arthur Jensen who plays an important role in Chapter 2 has recently died. What a great loss. I wish to acknowledge his indispensible role as a keen critic of my ideas who always looked to evidence rather than rhetoric. Who can take his place?

CHAPTER *1*

Our Genes and Ourselves

How much do our genes affect how we live? Addressing that theme will mean recapitulating material from my scholarly works. But the theme is important and something that I have not systematically discussed. I am writing to address the general reading public, but straight talk does not compromise anything I intend to say. As for specialists, they will, I hope, use the new data and material in Chapter 2 to clarify their thinking, and use the new method in Chapter 5 to go beyond kinship studies to measure the decay of family environment.

Everyone has heard generalizations, such as "our genes make us inherently violent," or "we are irrational by nature," or "the average person cannot hope to contribute much to human society." These are usually said in the context of denying the possibility of either human or personal progress. This book will test these assertions against history. If we have actually done something, such as become more rational, become more moral, made contributions to society beyond our so-called genetic potential, genes were powerless to forbid any of these things. You would think that our genes simply veto anything new. In fact, they have empowered us to progress our intelligence and moral rectitude toward limits as yet unknown. The quickest way to sell your soul is to keep saying "I cannot."

Genes are of great importance. Evidence shows that an individual's genes have a powerful influence on his or her life history. But not so powerful that individuals cannot choose to love both the truth and the good and thereby transcend the place on the human hierarchy at which their genes would "tend" to fix them. Particularly over the last 10,000 years, the collective genes of humanity have evolved away from a proclivity that favors violence and the principle of might makes right; and toward genes that allow a surprising degree of rationality and moral behavior. I call these two trends cognitive progress and moral progress, respectively, and try to show how they cross-fertilize. Throughout the evolution of our genes, there runs the domestication of the human species. We have tamed our genes (rather like taming domestic animals) as we have learned to live in larger societies. Throughout the pacification of our behavior, there runs the domestication of men by women. As the balance of power shifts toward women, the latter tame male violence more effectively.

1.1 OUTLINE OF THE CHAPTERS

The wonder is in the detail. Chapter 2 will defend the cognitive progress of humankind against criteria that purport to show that IQ gains are "hollow." New data about adults and children will drive the point home. It is followed by Appendix A, which adds background data and may be mainly of interest to specialists. Chapter 3 will look at dysgenics and eugenics: the thesis that current mating trends are sapping the quality of human genes so that, over the next few generations, hard-won progress will be lost. It will also look at whether the catastrophic events of recent history, such as the rule of Pol Pot in Cambodia, have depleted genes for cognition in various nations.

Chapter 4 will summarize moral progress. We have turned away from violence and cruelty toward humanity. It will also emphasize the role that cognitive progress has played in enhancing moral progress. Finally, it will pose challenges for the twenty-first century: our combination of reason and morality may not be able to solve problems that could reverse our evolving international society.

Chapter 5 will look at the role of genes in individual life history. At first, family environment, whether for good or ill, prevents the matching of genes and environment. However, it fades away at about the ages of 17−25. At that point, at whatever level of cognitive ability you choose, there is a tenuous matching of genes and environment for group achievement. This does not mean any individual's mind is immune to positive or negative environment. Our mental abilities are always subject to the shocks that adult life holds and the determination of individuals to hitch their star to thinking their way through life. An elegant new method will be used to make exact estimates of the age at which family environment fades. Appendix B follows this chapter. It spells out certain calculations in detail and once again, its contents will engage general readers only if they have a curiosity about such.

The last chapter will be a repeat of this introduction with the substance only detail can supply. It underlines a theme of my research: we must set aside the tendency to freeze the human mind and character in favor of assessing it as something adapted to whatever society it confronts. Since my research sets the stage for this book, I will spend the remainder of this chapter summarizing material from earlier works (Flynn, 2009, 2012) that new readers may find unfamiliar.

1.2 MASSIVE IQ GAINS OVER TIME

The record of how human beings have performed on IQ tests does more than measure us against one another for entry into Harvard law school. It provides priceless artifacts about how our minds have adapted from a simpler world to the world of modernity. We went from a society that posed mainly problems of how to manipulate the concrete world of everyday life for advantage (the utilitarian attitude) toward a society that expected us to classify, analyze abstract concepts, and take hypothetical situations seriously (the scientific attitude). They hint at a century of cognitive progress. Just as our cars altered because of modern science and the improved roads they traverse, so our minds have altered under the influence of modern schooling and the totality of the industrial revolution.

Take a Martian archeologist who lands on earth to investigate a ruined civilization. He finds the record of marksmanship contests held in 1865, 1998, and 1918. At each time, the tests may have been designed to see who had the keenest eyesight, the steadiest hand, and the best control over the weapon. But incredibly the average performance has escalated over time from 1 shot in the bull's-eye per minute, to 5 shots, to 50 shots. This would signal, of course, how much society had changed in terms of the weapons the average soldier used, from flintlock muskets to repeating rifles to machine guns. We have to imagine something more complex than tools. How did people's minds change to allow them to perform so much better on IQ tests, without any mechanical aids, but with what I call new habits of mind? How did their minds become equipped to deal with the content of IQ tests in terms of classifying objects, taking hypothetical situations seriously, and using logic on abstractions?

When Luria interviewed preindustrial peasants in Russia in the 1920s, he provided the answer. They did not classify. When he asked what a fish and crow had in common, they would not say that they were animals. One swims, one flies, you can eat one and not the other. They should not be lumped together because as objects in the concrete world, we use them differently. If you asked someone in 1900 what a rabbit and dog had in common, you use dogs to hunt rabbits. The fact that they were mammals was too incidental to be worthy of notice. They did not take the hypothetical seriously. When he asked them whether, granted that there were no camels in Germany, would there be camels in German cities, they said there must be camels if the city was large enough. When he asked them to reason about abstractions such as "wherever there is snow bears are white," "there is snow at the North Pole," "what color are the bears," they stayed firmly rooted in their experience of the concrete world. They had never seen anything but brown bears. But they might believe a reliable witness that came from the North Pole. In frustration, they asked Luria how they could solve problems that were not *real* problems.

We take classification, the hypothetical, reasoning about the abstract for granted. How do these new habits of mind explain how we function in the modern world?

Education has escalated from an average of some years of primary school to almost everyone having a high school diploma, plus over half of Americans with some tertiary education. It also teaches students differently. In 1910, children at the end of primary school took tests that asked almost entirely for socially valued concrete things: What were the capitals of the then-44 states? By 1990, the same children were asked to link abstract concepts in a chain of logic: Why is the largest city in a state often not the capital city? Because the rural state legislature hated the big cities and picked a county seat: Albany over New York city, Harrisburg over Philadelphia, Annapolis over Baltimore, and so forth. Needless to say, all courses that deal with modern science assume the scientific attitude: classifying, posing hypotheses, and linking abstractions with logic.

Work has become modernized. From only 3% of Americans working as professionals (doctor) or subprofessionals (teacher), we now find at least 35% earning their living as such. Not only are far more of them in conceptually demanding jobs, but also the jobs have been upgraded. Compare the banker of 1900 with the merchant bankers who, with incredible expertise about computers, financial markets, the conversion of debt into assets, brought down the financial world;

compare the tiller of the soil with the farm manager of today; compare the intuitive doctor of 1900 with today's scientifically-informed general practitioner, to say nothing of the medical specialist. As we shall see, even moral argument has been upgraded. We have gone from almost everyone just treating principles, despite all their cruelty, as concrete objects impervious to change (thou shalt not suffer a witch to live) toward people holding universal principles subject to correction by logic. For example, how can you reconcile your belief in justice with discriminating against people because they are black?

Today, there are IQ data from about 30 nations spread all over the world. It appears that shortly after a nation embarks on the industrial revolution, IQs begin to rise. Indeed, thanks to birth date data (scores rising as the subject's date of birth rises from the past to the present), we know that Britain has made massive IQ gains since 1872.

The industrial revolution demands a better educated work force, not just to fill new elite positions but to upgrade the average working person, progressing from literacy to grade school to high school to university. Women enter the work force. Better standards of living nourish better brains. Family size drops so that adults dominate the home's vocabulary and modern parenting develops (encouraging the child's potential for education). People's professions exercise their minds rather than asking for physically demanding repetitive work. Leisure at least allows cognitively-demanding activity rather than mere recuperation from work. The world's new visual environment develops so that abstract images dominate our minds and we can "picture" the world and its possibilities rather than merely describe it.

All of this may hint at a period of 100−150 years. At some date, a society begins to industrialize, enters the phase of massive IQ gains, and then these gradually dwindle away. Sooner or later, education is widespread and adequate, family size can go no lower, leisure is as packed with as many cognitively demanding pursuits and images as it can be, even featherbedding can produce no more elite jobs, and so the triggers of massive IQ gains stop. Some nations may pass through that cycle quicker than others.

For example, the developed world entered the cycle with Britain in 1850 and with China almost a century later on. Some nations, like the highly-educated and welfare states of Scandinavia, may have hit the optimum: their IQ gains may have ceased. Less progressive nations, such as America, the United Kingdom, Germany, and the nations of East Asia, such as Japan, China, and South Korea, are still in the IQ gains phase. The developing nations that have begun to develop, Argentina, Brazil, Turkey, and Kenya, are just entering their massive gains phase. Much of the world is still in the doldrums.

I have left the most important point to the last. It was the record of performance on IQ tests that led me to try to write cognitive history. Just what was it about the record that testified to the adaptation of minds to modernity? First we will look at the facts, then at the interpretation. Every nation in its IQ gains phase has made enormous gains on two kinds of tests. When the average person takes the mainline Wechsler or Stanford–Binet IQ tests, they score at 130 compared to the norms set 100 years ago. This puts the average person at that time at 70 against today's norms, or the cutting line for mental retardation. They were not retarded at all of course. No one needed the habits of mind of modernity to cope with that concrete world. When the average person takes Raven's Progressive Matrices, they score at 150 compared to the norms set 100 years ago (remember they were set by birth date data), which puts the average person at that time at 50 against today's norms.

Where have the Wechsler gains been the largest? First on the similarities subtest that forces you to classify. Second, on the analytic subtests that force you to use logic to devise how blocks or objects can make certain designs. Third, on the pictorial subtests which ask you to find the missing piece of a picture or use pictures to tell a story. Fourth, on the vocabulary subtest where adults made large gains thanks to more and more education. Children, of course, in recent years have had no more additional schooling, and their vocabulary gains have been modest.

Equally important, note that the Raven's gains are at least as huge as the most prominent Wechsler subtests, and they ask you to perceive logical sequences in highly abstract symbols. They are really a kind of analogies test. Fox and Mitchum (in press) brilliantly assess what has allowed each generation to do better than the preceding one.

There is no doubt that Americans 100 years ago could do simple analogies grounded in the concrete world: domestic cats are to wild cats as dogs are to what? (Wolves). By 1961, they could handle two squares followed by a triangle implies two circles followed by what? (A semicircle: just as a triangle is half of a square, so a semicircle is half of a circle). By 2006, they could handle two circles followed by a semicircle implies two 16s followed by what? (Eight: you have to see the relationship despite the transition from shapes to numbers). Note how each step takes us further from the concrete world toward using logic on abstractions, eventually abstractions whose very identity shifts. Who can imagine the average person in 1900 able to do all of that? Is it any wonder that we get much higher scores on Raven's?

In sum, the profiles match. Modernity means breaking from simply manipulating the concrete world for use. It means classifying, using logic on the abstract, pictorial reasoning, and more vocabulary. The IQ test items that have risen over time make the same cognitive demands. The enormous score gains are a symptom of the radically new habits of mind that distinguish us from our immediate ancestors.

1.3 THE DICKENS/FLYNN MODEL

The psychometric community initially rejected the notion that IQ gains entailed the enhancement of cognitive abilities that had counterparts in the real world. The culprit was environment. My hypothesis is that environmental triggers caused the gains; their hypothesis was that environment is too feeble to cause gains of real-world significance. As we will see in Chapter 2, this issue is not yet settled. But at present, I can at least demonstrate that environment is up to the task (Dickens & Flynn, 2001a, 2001b, 2002).

The twin studies focused on identical twins that were separated at birth and raised by different families. If they grew up with identical IQs, the inference was that identical genes had trumped dissimilar and enfeebled environments. If they grew up with IQs no more alike than the rest of us, dissimilar environment had trumped identical and enfeebled genes. The result: they were far more alike for IQ than randomly selected individuals. By adulthood, all kinship studies showed that family environment had faded away to zero. Adult IQs differed only to the degree that chance events might cause them to differ (one is dropped on his head and the other was not). It is hard to see how chance events could lead to massive IQ gains over time. (Well a few less might be dropped today, but how could that encourage analytic gains and discourage say arithmetic gains). They concluded that environment had so little potency to be a bad bet.

Let us see what happens to children that are genetically identical but grow up in different families. I will use basketball as an example. Joe and Jerry are identical twins separated at birth so that one is raised in Muncie Indiana and the other in Terre Haut. Thanks to their identical genes both will be 4 inches taller and a bit quicker than average (faster reflex arc). Indiana is a basketball mad state and at the start of school both boys get picked to play sandlot basketball more often than other kids. This is the beginning of matching above average genes with an above average environment. Moreover, there is reciprocal causation between their skills and their environment: better skills mean a better environment, which upgrades their skills, which means an even better environment, and so forth, essentially a feedback mechanism. The Dickens/Flynn model calls this the *individual multiplier*.

Next they make their grade school team and get regular play well beyond the average, which upgrades their skills further, and they both make their high school teams and get professional coaching. These separated twins will end up with highly similar basketball skills but why? Not merely because of their identical genes but also because of their highly similar basketball histories. In the kinship studies, genes get all the credit and basketball environment gets nothing. But this is a misinterpretation. It pretends that environment is feeble, when in fact their genes have co-opted something as potent as more play, team play, and professional coaching. Potent environment is disguised simply because it is matched with identical genes.

Now let us shift to factors that affect the collective basketball environment over time. The genes of people in general are essentially static over a few years, so now basketball environment is cut loose from genes and emerges in all its potency. After World War II, TV was invented and the close-ups of basketball were exciting and popularized the sport. Far more people participated and this raised the skill level. Indeed the rising average performance became a causal factor in its own right and a new feedback mechanism was born, which we call the *social multiplier*.

To be above average, it was initially good enough to shoot and pass well. Then ambidextrous people began to pass with either hand and find more open players, and their rising mean forced everyone who wanted to keep up to do the same. Then people began to shoot with either hand and get more opportunity to score baskets because they could go around a guard on either the right or left side. Almost overnight basketball was transformed from the stodgy sport of 1950 to the incredibly fluid and graceful sport that took root in the 1960s.

The comparative potency of genes or environment depended on whose hand was on the throttle of a multiplier. In competition over an individual's life history, genes co-opted environment and the individual's genes seemed omnipotent, thanks to the individual multiplier. In collective competition over time, evolving environment broke free to raise the average performance in basketball to new heights, thanks to the social multiplier.

I take it the analogy is obvious. Identical twins in separated environments may have genes that set them above (or below) the average person for cognitive ability. If above, what are small genetic differences at birth become potent because they co-opt matching and superior cognitive environments: more attentive teachers, superior peer interaction, honor streams, better high schools and universities, factors hardly rendered impotent simply because they are co-opted by genes. Over time, things are different. Increasing the years of schooling from 8 to 12 to more than 12 (university) really does do something to enhance the cognitive abilities of the whole society.

The same multipliers are at work. The near identical scores of separated identical twins do not rob environment of its potency. The huge environmentally-induced IQ gains over time do not rob genes of their potency. They are both potent enough to do their jobs: explaining individual differences versus explaining group differences over time. Environment is always potent, all the kinship studies not withstanding.

The multipliers solve a problem that had long baffled the psychological community. If environment was weak within groups, then to explain huge environmental effects between generations over time, you seemed to have to invent a factor X, a mysterious factor that operated exclusively between groups or generations. We now see that much the same factors are operating within and between groups. Within groups, individuals are distinguished by factors, such as better families, teachers, peers, universities, and jobs. But these factors are made to seem feeble because the individual multiplier correlates them with genetic differences and twin studies show them as having little impact beyond what genetic differences would dictate. Between groups, the two generations are also distinguished by better parenting, more schooling, and more cognitively demanding jobs. But thanks to the social multiplier, they have huge effects simply as environmental variables. They are operating free of genes because there are no genetic differences between the generations that they *could* be correlated with.

Much the same environmental factors operate both within and between groups and no mysterious factor X is necessary. This does not rule out some factors that may be more typical of one than the other.

1.4 MEASURING SOMETHING NEW

The cognitive history of the twentieth century was hidden in the record of performance on IQ tests. But the archeologist had to think about the people who actually got more correct answers. About how they thought in the test room; about how their minds had altered from one generation to another; and about how their genes interacted with environment, not only when individuals matched their own personal environment but also when a new environment affected individuals collectively.

Is it so odd that IQ tests began to measure the new traits and habits of mind that have evolved since 1850? You measure something when society decides it is valuable enough to measure. When people started to work at dawn and stopped at dusk, what was the need for a personal timepiece? But when the industrial revolution required people to get to work on time, we invented the factory whistle, the clock on the mantle, and the wristwatch. When people inherited their jobs as they did their names, what was the need for an IQ test? But when the industrial revolution required a more educated work force, we invented a measure of who could profit from education, who could progress farthest, and who could become the elite of the modern world. In 1905, Alfred Binet invented the IQ test. French school children told him that something new was worth measuring.

REFERENCES

Dickens, W. T., & Flynn, J. R. (2001a). Great leap forward: A new theory of intelligence. *New Scientist, 21*, 44–47.

Dickens, W. T., & Flynn, J. R. (2001b). Heritability estimates versus large environmental effects: The IQ paradox resolved. *Psychological Review, 108*, 346–369.

Dickens, W. T., & Flynn, J. R. (2002). The IQ paradox is still resolved: Reply to Loehlin and Rowe and Rodgers. *Psychological Review, 109*, 764–771.

Flynn, J. R. (2009). *What is intelligence? Beyond the Flynn effect.* Cambridge UK: Cambridge University Press (Expanded paperback edition).

Flynn, J. R. (2012). *Are we getting smarter: Rising IQ in the twenty-first century.* Cambridge UK: Cambridge University Press.

Fox, M. C., & Mitchum, A. L. (in press). A knowledge based theory of rising scores on "culture-free" tests. *Journal of Experimental Psychology: General.* Doi:10.1037/a0030155.

CHAPTER 2

Genes and Cognitive Progress

Those who think that environment is too feeble to cause massive IQ gains over time are mistaken. However, they have a fall-back position. They claim that it is precisely because IQ gains have been caused by altering environment that they lack real-world significance. Even if that were true, human beings might have made cognitive progress in the real world anyway. But my attempt to use the pattern of IQ gains as a tool to write the history of cognitive progress would go astray.

In 1998, when Arthur Jensen published *The g factor*, he offered what he called the method of "correlated vectors." He recommended it as a criterion for evaluating the significance of IQ gains over time. He ranked IQ tests from those that had the greatest "*g* loading" down to those that had the least; and he then ranked the same tests from those whose score gains were the greatest down to those whose score gains were least. He wanted to find whether the score gains tallied or correlated with "*g*". We will see why in a moment. But if you assume that *g* represents intelligence, this seemed a good way to discover whether IQ gains were really intelligence gains. He often used the subtests of the WISC (an abbreviation for Wechsler Intelligence Scale for Children) and the WAIS (an abbreviation for Wechsler Adult Intelligence Scale). These consist of 10−11 subtests. Their *g* loadings vary from vocabulary (usually the highest *g* loading) to coding (usually the lowest). If the subtest hierarchy of score gains tallied perfectly with their hierarchy of *g* loadings, the correlation would be 1.00. If the two hierarchies had nothing in common, the correlation would be zero.

2.1 JENSEN'S METHOD

If we reflect for a few moments, we can see why Jensen thought the method appropriate. There is nothing mysterious about *g* or the general intelligence factor. Something similar exists in many areas. All of us recognize that some people have "musical *g*": whatever instrument they pick up, they learn quickly. Other have "athletic *g*": they shine at all sports. There is a strong tendency for the same people to score above or below average on all of the 10 or 11 Wechsler subtests, no matter whether they test for vocabulary, general information, mental arithmetic, solving three-dimensional jigsaw puzzles, or discerning logical relations conveyed by a matrix. Factor analysis measures the strength of this "general intelligence factor." You can then go back to the subtests and calculate a hierarchy as to how much performance on each of them predicts general performance across the whole set of subtests. This is their g loading. The best predictor is usually (not always) your performance on the vocabulary subtest.

The impressive thing about the g loadings of subtests is that they rise with the degree of cognitive complexity of the task the subtests measure. As Jensen often pointed out, the g loading of Digit Span forward, a simple task of repeating a series of random numbers in the order in which they are read out, has a low g loading. Digit Span backward, a more complex task of saying numbers in reverse of the order in which they are read out, has a much higher g loading. Speed of shoe tying would have a g loading of close to zero. Most of us feel that the more cognitively complex a task the more it measures intelligence.

Therefore, Jensen's decision to use g as a substitute for the word "intelligence" seems sensible. And we now understand the reasons behind his decision to use the correlation between the hierarchy of score gains on subtests and the hierarchy of subtest g loadings as a criterion of significance. If the gains flunk, they do not seem to have much to do with general intelligence.

In 1998, when Jensen did this, he found no IQ gains data that gave a high positive correlation. Three sets gave modest correlations and he concluded that some increase in g was operative, although something else was involved as well. One set gave a negative correlation. He sums up by saying that IQ gains over time reflect g gains in part (he prefers to assign these to things like better nutrition creating better brains); and that they are in part "hollow." They may reflect only the acquisition of trivial skills like test sophistication. Test sophistication is the score boost someone gets simply because they have taken many IQ tests and have got used to the format. The part played in IQ gains by these hollow factors might differ randomly from one subtest to another, for example, they might be smaller for vocabulary with its high g loading and larger for coding with its low g loading. But they would all be trivial in terms of real-world significance.

Therefore, Jensen asserted that hollow score gains would have little if any payoff in real-life problem solving (Jensen, 1998, pp. 320–321, 332). His method has been influential (Colom, Garcia, Abad, & Juan-Espinoza, 2002; Colom, Garcia, Juan-Espinoza, & Abad, 2002; Deary & Crawford, 1998; Must, Must, & Raudik, 2003; Rushton, 1995; Woodley & Meisenberg, in press). Ruston and Jensen (2010) cite a comprehensive review that shows a negative correlation between IQ gains and g loadings.

The plausibility of the method was bolstered by the fact that it showed positive correlations between the g loading of subtests and the influence of genes on the same subtests. For example, inbreeding depression lowers performance on IQ subtests differentially. Inbreeding is known to have a deleterious effect on genes, and the more damage done by inbreeding on a subtest, the higher its g loading. Twin and kinship studies determine the relative impact of genes and environment on IQ subtests: the more individual differences in subtest performance were influenced by one's genetic inheritance, the higher the g loadings.

Thus Jensen forged a steel chain of ideas that fetters the minds of IQ specialists and makes them ignore the obvious (that the gains are important) for something peripheral (whether or not they tally with g). It also misleads them about causes: since the gains are "hollow," they must have hollow causes. Test sophistication is an ideal candidate because it only affects what goes on in the testing room and has little significance for the real world. Clearly whether you get a positive correlation between g and IQ gains plays a central role in Jensen's evaluation of the significance of IQ gains.

2.2 THE CONCEPTUAL FOUNDATIONS OF THE METHOD

Let us assess the case for the credentials of the method. When Wechsler subtests are ranked from largest to least in terms of their g loadings, the following are true: (i) the hierarchy correlates with the cognitive complexity of the task the subtests measure; (ii) the hierarchy correlates with the degree to which inbreeding (negatively) influences the subtests; and (iii) the hierarchy correlates with the heritability of the subtests, that is, the extent to which interpersonal differences are explained by genetic differences rather than environmental differences.

2.2.1 The Correlation Between *g* Loadings and Complexity

The first correlation is of great interest in itself. We must rely on our intuition to establish that the *g* hierarchy does correlate with the cognitive complexity of the task. But the case of digit span forward (simple and with a low *g* loading) and digit span backwards (more complex and with a higher *g* loading) is compelling. There is other evidence such as that making a soufflé has a higher *g* loading than scrambling eggs. Once we accept the relationship, it is illuminating. Vocabulary (assuming equal opportunity) ranks minds for the cognitive complexity of the concepts they can absorb. Arithmetic ranks them for how well they can plan a numerical strategy and carry it out mentally (without pen and paper). Which of the two involves more cognitive complexity? Vocabulary has the higher *g* loading—fascinating.

But the fact that the hierarchy of subtest *g* loadings is usually not correlated with the magnitude of IQ gains sheds no light on their causes or significance. Assume that the changing priorities of society drive IQ gains. The lack of correlation tells us only this: society picks and chooses between cognitive skills without reference to anything as socially irrelevant as the complexity of the task. The fact that since 1900, virtually everyone has become the pilot of a car has probably increased our mapping skills (low *g* loading). The fact that we today need to keep a lot of facts in mind to do our jobs may have increased our working memories (moderate *g* loading). The explosion of the percentage of Americans exposed to tertiary education has increased adult vocabularies and stores of general formation (high *g* loading). Which skill has made the greatest gain over time has nothing to do with their cognitive complexity. If vocabulary gains led (they do not), this would not be because of its high *g* loading, it would be because success at tertiary educations and the expansion of chattering jobs (lawyer, journalist) required more upgrading from vocabulary than from other cognitive skills.

Therefore, when we see some cognitive skill gain running ahead of others, the mere fact that such a thing occurs means we should do a sociological analysis to determine why. We do not need to determine whether the skill correlates with cognitive complexity. The brute fact of the difference in gains is enough. If too many people are being killed on the road, we might give compulsory driver training priority over more money for tertiary education. Therefore gains in mapping skills (with its low *g* loading) would be high, perhaps higher than vocabulary gains (with its high *g* loading). When we find the rare case in which IQ gains on subtests happen to tally with the cognitive complexity of the tasks, it is mainly an intriguing oddity.

The lack of correlation between *g* loadings and magnitude of gains certainly should not prejudice us in favor of trivial significance and trivial causes. Expanded adult vocabulary and stores of general information has huge social significance whatever its causes. The possibility that they are an illusion caused by growing test sophistication is remote. An adult American is presented with a word and has to offer a plausible definition. What has that to do with being accustomed to multi-choice tests? He has to place a city in the correct country or a country in the correct continent. Test sophistication is supposed to widen his knowledge of geography?

If anyone really thinks that test sophistication is responsible for score gains on these IQ subtests (rather than the spread of tertiary education), they should do the sociological hard yards. Present evidence that American adults have not really expanded these skills: data that when they use big words they are using them for show and without comprehension; or more seriously, that popular TV shows from the old *I Love Lucy* to the more recent *Hill Street Blues* do not evidence that the viewers have an expanded vocabulary or a higher level of general information.

The plausibility of test sophistication as a cause of gains on other subtests like Block Design or tests like Raven's Progressive Matrices is greater, of course. But we did not need Jensen's correlations to suggest the possibility. A dozen years before the method came into prominence, Flynn (1987) asked whether IQ gains had continued into eras when the population was saturated with multi-choice tests, and could hardly be assumed to be accumulating more test sophistication. They did. And now the method is supposed to show that the contrary is true?

2.2.2 The Correlation Between *g* Loadings and Inbreeding

I pass on to the fact that the hierarchy of *g* loadings correlates with the degree to which inbreeding (negatively) influences the subtests. This shows that those areas of the brain that do cognitively complex mental tasks have a genetic substratum more fragile than those areas that do less complex tasks. They are more subject to damage by the pairing of undesirable genes during sexual reproduction. That possibility, after all, is what inbreeding enhances.

This is interesting in itself as a contribution to our knowledge of brain physiology. But no one needed that discovery to explore whether increased outbreeding over time, people mating farther way from kin and thus lessening the bad effects of inbreeding, was a cause of IQ gains. My own investigation convinced me that in America at least, it made a small contribution during the nineteenth century and none during the twentieth. This is based on population flows from region to region and from abroad (Flynn, 2009b, 2012a). Jensen's method contributes nothing to how we assess the potency of this cause.

2.2.3 The Correlation Between *g* Loadings and Heritability

Finally, the hierarchy of subtest *g* loadings correlates with the heritability of the subtests, that is, the extent to which interpersonal IQ differences are predicted by genetic differences rather than differences in family environment. The kinship studies suggest (Jensen, 1998) that as people age, their IQ differences are more and more predictable from their genetic differences, and that their original differences in family environment (often called common environment) make less and less independent contribution. As people mature, and as the influence of their family fades versus peers and the larger society, the contribution of family environment trends toward zero by about the age 20.

But when they are school children, family environment is still active. The evidence shows that it has more impact on some subtests than others. The greater the cognitive complexity (*g* loading) of the subtest, the sooner a person's performance will attain a prefect match with his or her genetic potential. The match between genes and vocabulary may occur at age 20 and that for Digit Span not until say 24. This is fascinating and in Chapter 5, we will analyze evidence for the disappearance of family environment.

But the results have nothing to do with the significance or causes of IQ gains. At one time, it was thought that the fact that the environment seems so weak in explaining individual IQ differences meant that it must be too weak to cause IQ gains over time. But, as we have seen, the Dickens/Flynn model showed that the mathematics of heritability did not entail this (Dickens & Flynn, 2001a, 2001b, 2002). In addition, we also know that it is false from history. It may be that within a generation, genes can predict adult IQ far better than a person's years of education. But that does not mean that increasing the years of education enjoyed by everyone is too feeble to have a profound effect from one generation to another. The expansion of tertiary education has caused large adult gains on the vocabulary and information subtests.

2.2.4 Why the Method Carried Conviction

Psychology cannot ignore biology and some, particularly those alienated by the extreme environmentalism that prevailed in twentieth century social science, were convinced that psychology was ready to ignore Darwin. They interpreted his relevance as follows. Human traits alter by natural selection of genes favorable to that trait. It is true that natural selection is a response to environmental change, that is, some new environmental challenge makes those with certain genes, hitherto irrelevant or counterproductive, into individuals more likely to reproduce. Moths that are gray tend to be easy prey for birds, but then factory smoke blackens the air around cities and being gray has a survival value that spreads throughout the species. But it takes many generations for natural selection to alter the species, far too long to account for the escalation of IQ gains over a century.

Once you were focused on genes, genes the causes had to be, or more plausible, they had to be something rather like genes. By that I mean something that upgraded the brain to make it different from the brains of previous generations. If previous generations were poorly nourished, better diet nourished a new brain no longer crippled in terms of realizing its full potential. If previous generation were inbred, more outbreeding meant genetic changes in the next generation: changes that designed better brains. This ignores, of course, how much the social context can alter a human trait purely through "brain" exercise. Driving a taxi in London exercises the part of the brain that is the seat of mapping skills, even though taxi drivers have no genes that distinguish them from the average person. Those who take up weight lifting build up muscles that allow them to exceed the lifts of most people, genes being beside the point.

When Jensen's method "shows" that the causes of IQ gains are environmental, it would have some payoff if it showed just what environmental factors produced gains. Actually, its results cannot really discriminate even in favor of biological versus cultural. That question can only be decided by historical investigation. Look at the history of outbreeding from one generation to another and assess whether it could conceivably account for the magnitude of IQ gains over time. Look at the dietary record from one generation to another and see if it has the potency to explain whatever IQ gains occurred. The answer to both questions is negative. With the qualification that nutrition is active in the developing world and was active, even in advanced nations, before 1950 (Flynn, 2012a).

The real prejudice in favor of biological rather than cultural causes comes from the steel chain of ideas: the only real gains are those that tally with g (false); biological gains in isolation would tally with g because they upgrade the brain (perhaps true); therefore, the only real gains would be biologically caused ones (false premise, false conclusion).

2.2.5 Summary Judgment
Jensen's method reveals interesting things about the intellectual demands of tasks the Wechsler subtests measure, the fragility of the gene complexes (and brain centers) that underlie those tasks, and the speed with which aging attains a match between genes and environment. As a method of assessing the social significance or causes of IQ trends over time, it is irrelevant. Any possibility it suggests is already obvious. The case suggesting such a role has a flawed conceptual foundation and rests on ideology. Its continued application is a ritual that celebrates the ideology but has no scientific benefit.

2.3 THE METHOD IN PRACTICE

American adults made large gains on the vocabulary subtest, the equivalent of 17 IQ points, and sizable gains in general information, 8 IQ points, between 1953 and 2006. There have also been large adult vocabulary gains in Germany (Flynn, 2012a, Box 5 and Table A.I3). The gains on these subtests are obviously socially significant and very resistant to the influence of test sophistication. They are usually accompanied by gains on other subtests such that the total package of subtest gains lacks a positive correlation with the g loading hierarchy of those subtests. In other words, the package usually flunks Jensen's method. This should put an end to using that method to second guess both significance and causes. If we take it seriously, it suggests what we know to be false: that the vocabulary and information gains are "hollow" and probably due to test sophistication.

However, it is worth taking the method at its word, as a diagnostician of the significance and causes of score gains, and see where that leads: "By their fruits, ye shall know them" (Matthew 7:16).

When the vocabulary gains of American children (WISC gains from 1989 to 2002) are compared with those of American adults (WAIS gains from 1995 to 2006), they show a sharp contrast. When the method is applied to adults, it gives substantial positive correlations ranging from +0.540 to +0.621. When applied to their children, it gives negative correlations ranging from −0.303 to −0.409. (Specialists should look at Table A.1.) This poses an interesting series of causal problems. Adult gains were nonhollow and had genetic or biological causes. Child gains were hollow and had cultural causes, probably increased test sophistication.

Those who defend the method will need a lot of luck to salvage it. They can hardly contend that parents and their children are divided by some genetic gap. As for a biological gap, it is not very likely that adults upgraded their diets while cheating their children of the benefits (can fast-food school lunches come to the rescue here?). Does test sophistication end when you leave school, so it infects the gains of children and leaves significant the gains of adults? Even so, the adult gains are still significant and the child gains would presumably be the same if only test sophistication could be set aside.

2.3.1 The Exception
In singling out gains from the WAIS-III to the WAIS-IV, I have cherry picked an exception in that few other data sets would show a positive correlation with *g* loadings. That is true but why is it an exception? Table 2.1 gives the score gains on the eight WAIS subtests that were retained throughout the three periods of its existence. How certain subtests stood in the hierarchy of score gains within their set has been made explicit.

It is immediately apparent why WAIS-III to WAIS-IV period is an exception. Look at the entries in bold. Vocabulary and information are first and third among the subtests ranked from highest to lowest

Table 2.1 WAIS Subtest Gains Over Three Periods			
	WAIS to WAIS-R 1953–78	WAIS-R to WAIS-III 1978–95	WAIS-III to WAIS-IV 1995–2006
	Gains over 24.5 years (SD = 3)	Gains over 17 years (SD = 3)	Gains over 11 years (SD = 3)
Information	**1.1** (sixth)	**0.0** (next last)	**0.5** (third)
Arithmetic	1.0	−0.3	0.0
Vocabulary	**1.8** (first equal)	**0.6** (third equal)	**1.0** (first)
Comprehension	1.8	0.5	0.4
Picture completion	1.8	0.4	0.9
Block design	1.0	0.7	0.3
Object assembly	1.3	0.9	–
DS-coding	**1.8** (first equal)	**1.2** (first)	**0.2** (next last)
Picture arrangement	0.8	0.6	0.9
Source: *Adapted from Flynn, 2009a, Table 2—with permission of publishers of* Applied Neuropsychology. *See that table for sources and derivation of the estimates.*			

in terms of score gains. Apparently the effect of expanded tertiary education and verbally demanding jobs cast other influences in the shade in a way not replicated in earlier years. Since those two subtests have high g loadings, this created a positive correlation with g loadings.

It is true that only during the WAIS-III to WAIS-IV period are the score gains for these two subtests near the top. But who would cite that "chance" event as a reason to call its vocabulary and information gains real and all the others hollow. After all, the rates of gain on these two subtests were virtually the same in the early WAIS to WAIS-R period. Apparently, those gains are to be discounted because American adults made even higher gains elsewhere.

Also note the curse of gains on coding. Because it measures a skill with relative lack of complexity (how quickly you can copy symbols), it has a relatively low g loading. To make a substantial gain on this skill virtually doom gains, however large, on all the other subtests to insignificance. It is a pity we do not have data for speed of shoe tying that show huge gains. Then no score gains on all the Wechsler subtests could ever hope to qualify as real. But if people had shifted to wearing loafers and therefore no such gains occurred, all gains could hope for salvation.

Table 2.2 Correlations Between WAIS Subtest Gains and Subtest g Loadings When Coding Gains are put at Zero

	P1	S1	K1	K1(ad)	P2	S2	K2	K2(ad)
WAIS to WAIS-R	+0.495	+0.279	**+0.209**	**+0.319**	+0.690	+0.432	**+0.315**	**+0.516**
WAIS-R to WAIS-III	+0.137	+0.014	**+0.037**	**+0.080**	+0.341	+0.210	**+0.147**	**+0.220**
WAIS-III to WAIS-IV	+0.319	+0.524	**+0.386**	**+0.550**	+0.354	+0.401	**+0.315**	**+0.672**

P1 is Pearson with whatever g loadings are earlier.
S1 is Spearman with whatever g loadings are earlier.
K1 is Kendall with whatever g loadings are earlier.
K1(ad) is K1 adjusted for restriction of range.
P2 is Pearson with whatever g loadings are later.
S2 is Spearman with whatever g loadings are later.
K2 is Kendall with whatever g loadings are later.
K2(ad) is K2 adjusted for restriction of range.
Kendall's Tau-b values are in bold because they are to be preferred (Appendix A).

Table 2.2 drives the point home by setting coding gains at nil for all WAIS data sets. Like magic, the early WAIS to WAIS-R gains become positive, not as real as those for the later WAIS-III to WAIS-IV but still much improved. If only Wechsler had dropped coding from his battery, American adults would set an example of nonhollow IQ gains over most of a 53-year period. All correlations show positive values: as to why the Kendal correlations are to be preferred, see Appendix A.

2.3.2 Aid to Children

American children would still be remiss, of course. Let us see what we can do for them. Imagine a situation in which American children benefitted as much from extra formal education as American adults. The nation could not give them extra years of education as it did adults, but it went berserk with weekend tutoring. Every Saturday and Sunday, they attended sessions where they were forced to read demanding material and given lessons in Geography and History. As a result, they made substantial gains over time for vocabulary and general information.

Table 2.3 shows how tutoring might have affected American children. For the vocabulary and information subtests, it substitutes the large adult gains from the WAIS-III (1995) to the WAIS-IV (2002) in place of the minimal child gains from the WISC-IIII (1989) to the WISC-IV (2002).

	P1	S1	K1	P2	S2	K2
Table 2.3 WISC-III to WISC-IV Subtest Standard Score Gains Altered by Substitution of WAIS-III to WAIS-IV Vocabulary and Information Gains (for WISC Ones). When Altered, Half the Difference Between the WISC and WAIS Correlations is Eliminated						
WISC-III to WISC-IV (no substitutions)	−0.284	−0.389	−0.270	−0.333	−0.427	−0.341
WISC-III to WISC-IV (two substitutions)	+0.038	−0.079	−0.022	+0.068	−0.036	0.000
WAIS-III to WAIS-IV	+0.260	+0.462	+0.315	+0.316	+0.394	+0.333

Immediately the WISC gains go from strongly negative correlations to neutral. Which is to say that they move about half way toward the WAIS positive correlations. The effect is dramatic but clearly, there is still some difference, other than tertiary education, about social factors affecting American adults and children.

I suspect it is that adults have progressively shifted toward conceptually demanding jobs, while children's part-time work has remained rather basic (McDonald's). But the essential point is this: it is merely fortuitous that adult gains have, between the WAIS-III and WAIS-IV, mimicked g loadings. That is the odd thing. There is no obligation to explain why child gains have not. That is the normal state of affairs and there are innumerable social factors that would distinguish these children from these adults.

2.4 SUMMARY JUDGMENT

When applied, Jensen's method results in false positives (cases in which score gains happen to tally with g) that suggest pseudo-problems of causality. Luckily, this will be rare. Worse, it allows gains on some mental skills (coding) to rob gains on other mental skills of significance. Indeed, it allows them to undermine the significance of a whole battery of enhanced skills (which includes themselves!).

It might seem that adherents of the method could make a concession: although the Wechsler package flunks the test of g, gains on a few subtests like vocabulary and information could be significant. But any such concession is the beginning of the end. If we take the subtests one by one, they all have social significance. Tiny gains on arithmetic show that the schools are doing badly in that area, huge gains on similarities show that we are better at using abstract concepts to classify, big gains on block design show that our analytic abilities are improving, big gains on coding signal faster speed of information processing, and so forth. Whether the package passes the test of g is now irrelevant to its social significance. Whatever value g may have for understanding individual differences in intelligence, it fades out of the realm of cognitive history to be replaced by the concept of shifting social priorities.

One concession and the ballgame is over. One concession means that it is natural for society to evolve without some overall design of enhancing skills in accord with their cognitive complexity (g loadings). Dismissive comments about test sophistication are in order only if there is independent evidence for such. Sociology replaces mathematical models that rest on unstated assumptions about human behavior. Once stated, the assumption of Jensen's method carries no conviction: that there is a presence looming over history (g or true intelligence) that forbids the autonomous enhancement of various cognitive abilities.

As for diagnosing causes, one way of salvaging the method is to calibrate it into impotence. We can deny that positive and negative correlations are decisive, and interpret them as showing that a mix of genetic and cultural factors is at work. But that is a truism. We did not need the method to tell us that all IQ trends involve a mix. Both cultural and genetic trends are always active. Over the past century, the fact that gains are large tells us that cultural factors have been far more important. Positive cultural trends had to overwhelm negative genetic ones to yield a credit balance. To disentangle the two, we must use sociology. We calculate that dysgenic mating (people with less education "over" reproducing) would lower IQ by one point per generation. Given a 10-point gain that puts cultural factors at a positive effect of 11 points. If there were a 10-point loss, the negative effect of cultural factors would be 9 points.

2.4.1 Are Black IQ Gains Significant?

Jensen's method also clouds the question of what it means when the IQ gap between groups alters over time. For example, he stresses that black gains on whites over time flunk his method: the larger the g loading of the subtest, the smaller the black gains on whites. Therefore, black gains are not significant. On the other hand, the black versus white IQ deficit at any given time passes his method. For example, in 1972 or in 2002, the larger the *g* loading on a subtest, the bigger the black versus white score gap. Therefore, the racial IQ gap is truly significant.

Ruston and Jensen versus Dickens and Flynn debated black IQ gains on whites between 1972 and 2002. We put the gain at 4−7 IQ points. They interpreted our Wechsler−Binet data as implying a 3.44 gain and cited tests that gave lesser values: the Wonderlic Personnel Test at +2.4 points; the Kaufman Assessment Battery for Children at −1.0 points; and the Differential Ability Scale at a maximum of +1.83 points. The average gain is 1.67 points and they propose a range of nil to 3.44 points as their final estimate.

We defended our estimate at the time (Dickens & Flynn, 2006a, 2006b) but who is correct is not the point in this context. Let us assume that their 1.67 points is more probable than our 5.5 points. What is striking is that they did not defend any of the data sets they cited as ones that *had passed Jensen's criterion of significance*: as data that showed a positive correlation between the magnitude of black gains on subtests and the *g* loading of the subtests. In fact, they emphasize the fact that the secular increase is *not* on the *g* factor. They call this a finding that has been well replicated and, of course, cite it as evidence that black gains are hollow.

This means that the overall position of Jensen and Rushton is logically incoherent. They label the IQ difference between blacks and whites at any given time as *real* (the larger the racial gap by subtest, the higher the *g* loadings of the subtests, which gives a robust positive correlation). However, they label black gains on white over time as *hollow*. In sum, they believe three propositions: the black−white IQ gap in 1972 was significant and real; the black−white IQ gap of 2002 was significant and real; the IQ gains that reduced the gap were hollow and unreal.

The only way anyone can believe in all three of those propositions is to assume that a hollow cause can eliminate one reality and replace it with another. Awaiting such an argument, every apparent alteration of an IQ gap between groups in history, for example, the fact that women eliminated the advantage men once held on Raven's, either did not really occur or had hollow causes. Unless, of course, we find that the intervening IQ gains were an exception to the rule that most such have a negative correlation with *g*.

2.4.2 GQ Versus IQ

As Jensen's method is deceptive, we need a new way of assessing cognitive gains in the light of their correlations with *g*. The Woodcock–Johnson test supplies the correct method: weight the subtest gains by the size of their *g* loadings. The gain on vocabulary punches above its weight because it is multiplied by a high *g* loading. The gain on coding is discounted by multiplying it by a low *g* loading.

Table 2.4 shows that when black gained on whites (from the WISC-III to WISC-IV), they made subtest gains that had a sizable negative correlation with their *g* loadings. It also shows that this made little difference. The IQ gain is 5.00 points, the GQ gain is 4.72 points, and the difference is 0.28 points or 5.6%.

Table 2.4 WISC-III to WISC-IV Gains with WISC-IV *g* Loadings: GQ Versus IQ

	Gains	WISC-IV *g* Loadings	Gains × *g* Loadings	Divided by Ave *g* Loading
Symbol search	1.2	0.566	0.68	1.01
Block design	1.0	0.660	0.66	0.98
Picture completion	0.7	0.627	0.44	0.65
Similarities	0.7	0.798	0.56	0.83
Coding	0.7	0.466	0.33	0.49
Comprehension	0.4	0.716	0.29	0.43
Information	0.3	0.813	0.24	0.36
Vocabulary	0.1	0.836	0.08	0.12
Digit span	0.1	0.512	0.05	0.07
Arithmetic	−0.2	0.743	−0.15	−0.22
Totals & Ave.	**5.0**	0.6737	3.18	**4.72**

SS gains translated into IQ and GQ gains:
SS 5.0 = 5.0 IQ, SS 4.72 = 4.72 IQ; Difference = 0.28 points.
Equivalence table: Wechsler, 2003a, Table A.6.
Note: In this table, the values for score gains and g loadings have not been corrected by dividing them by the square root of the reliability coefficients of the subtests. When weighting scores for differences in g loadings, the latter are normally taken as given. Corrections make no difference to the point at issue, namely, how little difference weighting for g loadings makes.
Directions: You take the products and divide them by the average g loading. Then sum the standard score gains and go to the table that converts standard score totals into an IQ metric. This new GQ will be a bit less than the unweighted total that gives IQ.

2.4.3 Are Massive IQ Gains Over Time Significant?

Table 2.5 makes much the same assessment about America's massive IQ gains over time. It contrasts IQ and GQ gains for both the WISC (children) and WAIS (adults) over a whole half century. Cumulatively, the generally negative correlations for the WISC have lowered gains from 18.90 points (IQ) to 18.11 points (GQ), a decrease of −0.79 points or 4.2%. The positive correlations for the WAIS have raised gains from 16.09 (IQ) to 16.14 (GQ), an increase of +0.05 points or 0.3%. The concept of g is important. But in the real world of score gains over time, full-scale IQ is quite good enough. Corrections for g loadings are not really necessary.

What have we learned? We can now solve the riddle we posed: how hollow score gains over time can alter the real cognitive gap between groups. The "real gains" (expressed in GQ points) and the "hollow gains" (expressed in IQ points) are virtually identical. And this is true no matter whether the rank order correlation of gains with g loadings is positive or negative. The reason for this is that the g loadings of all the Wechsler subtests differ only slightly and therefore, weighting for them has little effect. The g loading of all the subtests is also heavy.

Table 2.5 Comparing IQ and GQ Gains WISC to WISC-IV and WAIS to WAIS-IV			
	WISC	**WISC-R**	**WISC-III**	**WISC-IV**
SS total unweighted	100.00	111.63	118.90	123.90
SS total g weighted	100.00	111.30	118.39	123.11
IQ	100.00	108.63	114.90	118.90
GQ	100.00	108.30	114.39	118.11
GQ minus IQ	0.00	−0.33	−0.51	−0.79
	WAIS	**WAIS-R**	**WAIS-III**	**WAIS-IV**
SS total unweighted	100.00	114.60	119.69	124.09
SS total g weighted	100.00	114.60	119.58	124.14
IQ	100.00	109.60	112.69	116.09
GQ	100.00	109.60	112.58	116.14
GQ minus IQ	0.00	0.00	−0.11	+0.05

I have used the WISC-IV and WAIS-IV conversion tables as a common metric because they are similar in format. Those who check the calculations should note that some subtest totals are for 11 subtests while the conversion tables assume 10 and they must prorate accordingly. The above uses the prorated values. Equivalence tables: Wechsler, 2003a, Table A.6; Wechsler, 2008a, Table A.7.

If blacks gain on whites on a set of tasks *all of which* involve considerable cognitive complexity, is it any wonder that their gains turn out to be significant even in the light of *g*?

2.4.4 Philosophers and Psychometricians

It took philosophers to invent the problem of scientific realism, question whether or not science informs us about the nature of the external world (Flynn, 2012b). It took psychometricians to invent the problem of "hollow" gains, question whether or not massive IQ gains inform us about cognitive progress over the last century.

Today it is usual rather than rare to have some tertiary education. Today 35% of us, rather than a handful, are professionals or subprofessionals, high-level or low-level managers, technicians or lab assistants, and members of the chattering classes, i.e., lawyers, journalists, teachers, writers, counselors, and media people. Today women, thanks to greater exposure to modernity, have closed the IQ gap with men. Today blacks, due to better educational and employment opportunities, have eliminated one-third of their IQ (and GQ) gap with whites.

Yet we are supposed to have no larger vocabularies or funds of general information than the village blacksmiths, factory hands, and upstate New York farmers that were our ancestors. Blacks are supposed to have made no meaningful IQ gains on whites because their gains are not *g* gains. I have a suspicion as to why no one has applied the method to the gains of women. It would be embarrassing to have to contend that the fact that women now match men for IQ is not meaningful. I believe that there has been cognitive progress over the last century. But Jensen's method purports to show how misguided I am.

Once our minds are liberated, we can appreciate the majesty of the cognitive history of the last century. Persistent escalation of years of education set into motion feedback mechanisms that produced large vocabulary gains over time. As better-educated people developed larger vocabularies, the new and better vocabulary environment affected everyone, even those outside tertiary institutions (their spouses, friends, clients). Every person that responded to the initial increase in mean vocabulary boosted the mean further, which affected every individual anew, and away you go.

Larger vocabularies had a spillover into other cognitive abilities but not in accord with their degree of cognitive complexity. Vocabulary gains quite naturally fed gains in using words to classify (similarities) but had almost no affect on mental arithmetic. The fact that similarities have made even larger gains than vocabulary shows that it profited not only from vocabulary spillover but also from its own exogenous trigger (Flynn, 2012a). Sadly, extra years of education did not trigger much of a rise in arithmetical abilities. Our pedagogy is missing something here.

However, let us end on a positive note. We have gone from hewers of wood and drawers of water to a population among whom those who perform cognitively and verbally demanding work may soon become a majority. How many in 1900 would have thought such a thing possible? The history of the American mind over the last century is not a tale of something hollow. It is the story of great intellectual potential realized in ordinary people.

REFERENCES

Colom, R., Abad, F. J., Garcia, L. F., & Juan-Espinosa, M. (2002). Education, Wechsler's full scale IQ, and g. *Intelligence, 30*, 449–462.

Colom, R., Garcia, L. F., Juan-Espinosa, M., & Abad, F. J. (2002). Null sex differences in general intelligence: Evidence from the WAIS-III. *Spanish Journal of Psychology, 5*, 29–35.

Deary, I. J., & Crawford, J. R. (1998). A triarchic theory of Jensenism: Persistent, conservative, reductionism. *Intelligence, 26*, 273–282.

Dickens, W. T., & Flynn, J. R. (2001a). Great leap forward: A new theory of intelligence. *New Scientist, 21*, 44–47.

Dickens, W. T., & Flynn, J. R. (2001b). Heritability estimates versus large environmental effects: The IQ paradox resolved. *Psychological Review, 108*, 346–369.

Dickens, W. T., & Flynn, J. R. (2002). The IQ paradox is still resolved: Reply to Loehlin and Rowe and Rodgers. *Psychological Review, 109*, 764–771.

Dickens, W. T., & Flynn, J. R. (2006a). Black Americans reduce the racial IQ gap: Evidence from standardization samples. *Psychological Science, 17*, 913–920.

Dickens, W. T., & Flynn, J. R. (2006b). Common ground and differences. *Psychological Science, 17*, 923–924.

Flynn, J. R. (1987). Massive IQ gains in 14 nations: What IQ tests really measure. *Psychological Bulletin, 101*, 171–191.

Flynn, J. R. (2009a). The WAIS-III and WAIS-IV: Daubert motions favor the certainly false over the approximately true. *Applied Neuropsychology, 16*, 1–7.

Flynn, J. R. (2009b). *What is intelligence? Beyond the Flynn effect*. Cambridge UK: Cambridge University Press. (Expanded paperback edition).

Flynn, J. R. (2012a). *Are we getting smarter: Rising IQ in the twenty-first century*. Cambridge UK: Cambridge University Press.

Flynn, J. R. (2012b). *Fate and philosophy: A journey through life's great questions.* Wellington, New Zealand: AWA Press.

Jensen, A. R. (1998). *The g factor: The science of mental ability.* New York: Praeger.

Must, O., Must, A., & Raudik, V. (2003). The secular rise in IQs: In Estonia, the Flynn effect is not a Jensen effect. *Intelligence, 31*, 461−471.

Rushton, J. P. (1995). *Race, evolution, and behavior: A life history perspective.* New Brunswick NJ: Transaction Publishers.

Rushton, J. P., & Jensen, A. R. (2010). The rise and fall of the Flynn effect as a reason to expect a narrowing of the Black/White IQ gap. *Intelligence, 38*, 213−219.

Wechsler, D. (1949). *Wechsler intelligence scale for children: Manual.* New York: The Psychological Corporation.

Wechsler, D. (1955). *Wechsler adult intelligence scale: Manual.* New York: The Psychological Corporation.

Wechsler, D. (1974). *Wechsler intelligence scale for children—revised.* New York: The Psychological Corporation.

Wechsler, D. (1981). *Wechsler adult intelligence scale—revised.* New York: The Psychological Corporation.

Wechsler, D. (1992). *Wechsler intelligence scale for children—third edition: Manual.* San Antonio, TX: The Psychological Corporation. (Australian adaptation).

Wechsler, D. (1997). *Wechsler adult intelligence scale—third edition: Technical and interpretive manual.* San Antonio, TX: The Psychological Corporation.

Wechsler, D. (2003a). *Wechsler intelligence scale for children—fourth edition: Manual.* San Antonio, TX: The Psychological Corporation. (Australian adaptation).

Wechsler, D. (2003b). *The WISC-IV technical manual.* San Antonio, TX: The Psychological Corporation.

Wechsler, D. (2008a). *Wechsler adult intelligence scale—fourth edition: Manual.* San Antonio, TX: Pearson.

Wechsler, D. (2008b). *Wechsler adult intelligence scale—fourth edition: Technical and interpretive manual.* San Antonio, TX: Pearson.

Woodley, M. A., & Meisenberg, G. (in press). In the Netherlands the anti-Flynn effect is a Jensen effect. *Personality and Individual Differences.* doi:10.1016/j.paid.2012.12.022.

APPENDIX A (PRIMARILY FOR SPECIALISTS)

The text promised detail about adult versus child gains. Table A.1 isolates the vocabulary gains of American children (WISC: from 1989 to 2002) and those of American adults (WAIS: from 1995 to 2006) and applies the method of correlated vectors to both. The contrast is striking: adults show substantial positive correlations and their children negative correlations. Therefore, according to the method of correlated vectors, adult IQ gains are significant and the gains of their own children are hollow. Kendall's Tau-b (ad) values are in bold because they are to be preferred.

Table A.1 WISC-III to WISC-IV and WAIS-III to WAIS-IV: Compared for Correlations Between Subtest Gains and Subtest g Loadings								
	P1	**S1**	**K1**	**K1(ad)**	**P2**	**S2**	**K2**	**K2(ad)**
WISC-III to WISC-IV	−0.284	−0.389	−0.270	**−0.302**	−0.333	−0.427	−0.341	**−0.409**
WAIS-III to WAIS-IV	+0.260	+0.462	+0.315	**+0.621**	+0.316	+0.394	+0.333	**+0.540**
Difference	0.540	0.851	0.585	**0.923**	0.649	0.821	0.674	**0.949**

P1 is Pearson with whatever g loadings are earlier.
S1 is Spearman with whatever g loadings are earlier.
K1 is Kendall with whatever g loadings are earlier.
K1(ad) is K1 adjusted for restriction of range.
P2 is Pearson with whatever g loadings are later.
S2 is Spearman with whatever g loadings are later.
K2 is Kendall with whatever g loadings are later.
K2(ad) is K2 adjusted for restriction of range.

Understanding Table A.1

To assess the correlations in Table A.1 some comment is needed. When you compare the hierarchy of score gains on subtests to see if they tally with subtest g loadings, you can calculate three different correlation coefficients: the Pearson, the Spearman, and Kendall's Tau-b. I have offered all three but the Kendall is to be preferred. With only 10 or 11 pairs in the hierarchy, the Pearson is too sensitive to one atypical pair (an outlier). The Spearman gives inflated correlations when you have tied pairs. The Kendal corrects for this fault. The reason there are two sets of correlations for each scores gain is this. When calculating whether WISC-III to WISC-IV score gains tally with subtest g loadings, I did not want to choose between using the g loadings for the WISC-III and the WISC-IV. So I used both g loadings (called "earlier" and "later") and calculated the three kinds of correlations using each in turn.

Then there is the adjustment of the preferred or Kendall correlations for restriction of range. As Jensen (1998) points out, all correlations are reduced by the fact that the g loadings of the Wechsler subtests vary only from about +0.400 to +0.900. This covers only a small part of the total range of possible g loadings, from shoe tying that would be close to zero and a super-Raven's test that would be close to 1.00. It is as if a sample restricted to tall people was used to calculate the correlation between height and weight.

In Table A.1, the adjustments for restriction of range dramatize the contrast between adults and children. The Kendall values for the

WISC rise from $-0.270/-0.341$ to $-0.302/-0.409$. The Kendall values for the WAIS rise from $+0.315/+0.333$ to $+0.621/+0.540$. The final contrast is 0.923 or 0.949. Extraordinary—it is as if the adults and children came from radically different populations.

Background Data for Table A.1

Table A.1 rests on a series of tables. To apply the method of correlated vectors, we must have: (i) a hierarchy of WISC subtests with their g loadings for each time they were administered; (ii) a hierarchy of WISC subtests with their score gains for each time; (iii) a hierarchy of WAIS subtests with their g loadings for each time they were administered; and (iv) a hierarchy of WAIS subtests with their score gains for each time. For each period, say score gains from the WISC to WISC-R, I have given both sets of values described above. You can choose either using the earlier WISC g loadings (at the beginning of the period) or the later WISC-R g loadings (at the end of the period). To adjust the score gains during that period, see Tables A.2–A.5.

Table A.2 WISC Subtest g Loadings (Corrected for Subtest Reliabilities)						
	WISC	WISC-R	WISC-R	WISC-III	WISC-III	WISC-IV
Vocabulary	0.861	0.913	0.866	0.856	0.859	0.889
Information	0.878	0.843	0.826	0.847	0.847	0.874
Arithmetic	0.798	0.714	0.731	0.798	0.813	0.790
Comprehension	0.832	0.844	0.799	0.775	0.785	0.796
Similarities	0.765	0.841	0.844	0.861	0.861	0.858
P. arrangement	0.754	0.681	0.671	0.615	—	—
Block design	0.671	0.780	0.777	0.755	0.718	0.710
Object assem.	0.682	0.735	0.712	0.741	—	—
P. completion	0.641	0.708	0.683	0.702	0.669	0.682
Coding	0.543	0.482	0.485	0.394	0.443	0.507
Digit span			0.525	0.497	0.511	0.551
Symbol search					0.644	0.636

Sources of subtest intercorrelations (uncorrected):
WISC (Wechsler, 1949, Tables 4 and 5),
WISC-R (Wechsler, 1974, Table 15),
WISC-III (Wechsler, 1992, Table C.12),
WISC-IV (Wechsler, 2003b, Table 5.12).
Sources of subtest reliability coefficients (to make corrections):
WISC (Wechsler, 1949, Table 7),
WISC-R (Wechsler, 1974, Table 9),
WISC-III (Wechsler, 1992, Table 5.1),
WISC-IV (Wechsler, 2003b, Table 4.1).

Table A.3 WISC Subtest Standard Score Gains (Corrected for Subtest Reliabilities)

	WISC to WISC-R	WISC to WISC-R	WISC-R to WISC-III	WISC-R to WISC-III	WISC-III to WISC-IV	WISC-III to WISC-IV
Similarities	3.24	3.06	1.44	1.44	0.78	0.75
Coding	2.84	2.65	0.82	0.79	0.79	0.76
Object assem.	1.70	1.62	1.43	1.45	—	—
Block design	1.38	1.39	0.98	0.97	1.08	1.08
Comprehension	1.48	1.48	0.68	0.68	0.45	0.44
P. arrangement	1.10	1.09	2.22	2.18	—	—
P. completion	0.94	0.86	1.02	1.02	0.80	0.76
Vocabulary	0.42	0.43	0.43	0.43	0.11	0.11
Information	0.51	0.48	−0.33	−0.33	0.33	0.32
Arithmetic	0.42	0.41	0.34	0.34	−0.23	−0.21
Digit span			0.11	0.11	0.11	0.11
Symbol search					1.38	1.35

Sources of gains (unadjusted):
Digit span (Wechsler, 1992, Table 6.8 and Wechsler, 2003b, Table 5.8),
Symbol search (Wechsler, 2003b, Table 5.8),
All others (Flynn, 2012a, Table A.II3).
Sources of subtest reliability coefficients (to make adjustments)—see Table A.2.

Table A.4 WAIS Subtest *g* Loadings (Corrected for Subtest Reliabilities)

	WAIS	WAIS-R	WAIS-R	WAIS-III	WAIS-III	WAIS-IV
Vocabulary	0.893	0.880	0.875	0.879	0.878	0.844
Information	0.921	0.865	0.861	0.849	0.845	0.784
Arithmetic	0.799	0.835	0.810	0.778	0.795	0.771
Comprehension	0.886	0.849	0.849	0.862	0.853	0.840
Similarities	0.847	0.858	0.854	0.873	0.866	0.854
P. arrangement	0.925	0.814	0.738	0.769	—	—
Block design	0.783	0.811	0.767	0.752	0.722	0.686
Object assem.	0.776	0.792	0.728	0.735	—	—
P. completion	0.838	0.784	0.768	0.695	0.669	0.623
Coding	0.710	0.668	0.657	0.585	0.642	0.656
Digit span			0.666	0.558	0.577	0.687
Symbol search					0.784	0.628

Sources of subtest intercorrelations (uncorrected):
WAIS (Wechsler, 1955, Tables 8 and 9),
WAIS-R combined with the WAIS (Wechsler, 1981, Table 15, ages 35–44),
WAIS-R combined with the WAIS-III (Wechsler, 1981, Table 16, nine ages),
WAIS-III (Wechsler, 1997, Table 4.12),
WAIS-IV (Wechsler, 2008b, Table 5.1).
Sources of subtest reliability coefficients (to make corrections):
WAIS (Wechsler, 1955, Table 6),
WAIS-R combined with the WAIS (Wechsler, 1981, Table 10, ages 35–44),
WAIS-R combined with the WAIS-III (Wechsler, 1981, Table 10, nine ages),
WAIS-III (Wechsler, 1997, Table 3.1),
WAIS-IV (Wechsler, 2008b, Table 4.1).

Table A.5 WAIS Subtest Standard Score Gains (Corrected for Subtest Reliabilities)						
	WAIS to WAIS-R (1)	WAIS to WAIS-R (2)	WAIS-R to WAIS-III (1)	WAIS-R to WAIS-III (2)	WAIS-III to WAIS-IV (1)	WAIS-III to WAIS-IV (2)
Similarities	2.39	2.39	0.98	0.97	0.75	0.75
Coding	1.87	1.96	1.33	1.30	0.22	0.22
Comprehension	2.04	1.96	0.54	0.54	0.43	0.43
P. completion	1.96	1.96	0.44	0.44	0.99	0.98
Vocabulary	1.84	1.84	0.61	0.62	1.04	1.03
Object assem.	1.57	1.52	1.09	1.07	—	—
Information	1.15	1.16	0.00	0.00	0.52	0.52
Arithmetic	1.10	1.08	−0.33	−0.32	0.00	0.00
Block design	1.10	1.06	0.75	0.75	0.32	0.32
P. arrangement	1.00	0.91	0.70	0.70	—	—
Digit span			0.11	0.11	0.32	0.31
Symbol search					0.11	0.11

Sources of uncorrected subtest score gains:
Symbol search (Wechsler, 2008b, Table 5.5); all others (Flynn, 2012a, Table A.II2).
Sources of subtest reliability coefficients (to make corrections)—see Table A.4.

Arithmetic

If you merely wish to check the accuracy of the correlations in Table A.1, using the method of correlated vectors, the corrected values in Tables A.2–A.5 will be sufficient. If you wish to verify the arithmetic used to correct for differences in subtest reliability, you will have to divide all uncorrected gains and *g* loadings by the square root of the subtest reliability coefficients. The sources are at the bottom of the relevant tables but a preview of what you will encounter may help. The main problem is the paucity of the early data.

The WISC data give intercorrelations between subtests only for ages 7½ and 10½. You will have to calculate the uncorrected *g* loadings from these. The data also give subtest reliability coefficients for both of these two ages: you will first have to use the square roots of these as divisors and then average the results. The WISC to WISC-R gains extend over all ages. However, as you wish to correlate the gains with both WISC and WISC-R *g* loadings, you will have to average the WISC-R reliability coefficients for ages 7½ and 10½ to get the first and use the average for all ages to get the second. After that, it is straightforward.

The WAIS to WAIS-R data give IQ gains not for all adults but uses a group of 35–44 year olds. You will find no subtest reliability coefficients for those ages, but there are ones for ages 25–34 and 45–54. So these will have to be averaged to get the divisor you want. Because the WAIS to WAIS-R gains extend over ages 35–44 and the WAIS-R to WAIS-III gains cover all ages, you will again need two sets of reliability coefficients: the WAIS-R coefficients for ages 35–44; and the average of the WAIS-R coefficients for all ages. After that, it is straightforward.

How to Adjust for Restriction of Range

I have already defended calculating the adjustments for restriction of range in my comments on Table A.1. Most studies do not do this but it is essential. Some sets of *g* loadings have an SD more than twice the size of others. This makes a huge difference in the magnitude of the unadjusted correlations and therefore, they are simply not comparable. Note that *both* gains and subtest *g* loadings were corrected for the fact that subtests have varying reliability. All values were divided by the square root of the reliability coefficients.

The simplest method of adjusting for restriction of range is to simply calculate the SD of the values for *g* loadings, which gives you the sample SD. The population is defined as having *g* loadings ranging from 0.001 to 0.999 with a normal distribution: its SD is 0.167. You already have the correlation within the restricted sample. These three values are then fed into the standard formula.

As a check, I used a second method which is illustrated by an example. Case selected: the correlation between the WAIS-III to WAIS-IV gains on subtests and the *g* loadings of subtests (using WAIS-IV *g* loadings).

1. The relevant WAIS-IV *g* loadings range from 0.623 to 0.854. These values are assumed to take their positions on a normal distribution where the median would be 0.500. Therefore, the sample range runs from 0.74 SDs above the median to 2.12 SDs above the median: $0.123/0.167 = 0.74$ and $0.354/0.167 = 2.12$.
2. Therefore, the sample covers from the 77.04 to 98.30 percentiles, with the bottom 77.04% missing and the top 1.70% missing. The missing top percentage reduces the SD of a normal curve by 0.048 and the bottom missing percentage reduces the SD by 0.480. The total lost is 0.528, which means the sample SD is 0.472 of the population SD.

3. We now have the values needed to adjust: sample correlation = +0.333; sample SD = 0.472; population SD = 1.000. The population SD is now been set at 1 because the sample SD is expressed as a decimal (0.472 of the population SD).
4. Substituting these values into the standard formula raises unadjusted +0.333 to adjusted +0.599 (for WAIS-III to WAIS-IV).

Adjusted Values for Restriction of Range

Table A.1 highlights values that are adjusted for restriction of range, so as to contrast the negative correlations for children (WISC) and the positive correlations for adults (WAIS) during roughly the same period: from 1992 (1989 and 1995) to 2004 (2002 and 2006). I have used only the first method because the second gives results so close as to make no real difference. To allow the reader to compare, Table A.6 gives values that are unadjusted, adjusted using method 1, and adjusted using method 2. The method 1 adjusted values in bold are, of course, the ones contained in Table A.1.

Table A.6 From Table A.1, Kendall's Tau-b Correlations Unadjusted and As Corrected by Either Method 1 or Method 2

	Unadjusted	Method 1	Method 2
WISC-III to WISC-IV (WISC-III g loadings)	−0.270	**−0.302**	−0.408
WISC-III to WISC-IV (WISC-IV g loadings)	−0.341	**−0.409**	−0.523
WAIS-III to WAIS-IV (WAIS-III g loadings)	+0.315	**+ 0.621**	+0.548
WAIS-III to WAIS-IV (WAIS-IV g loadings)	+0.333	**+ 0.540**	+0.599

Table A.7 From Table 2.2, Kendall's Tau-b Correlations Unadjusted and As Corrected by Either Method 1 or Method 2

	Unadjusted	Method 1	Method 2
WAIS to WAIS-R (WAIS g loadings)	+0.209	**+ 0.319**	+0.462
WAIS to WAIS-R (WAIS-R g loadings)	+0.315	**+ 0.516**	+0.644
WAIS-R to WAIS-III (WAIS-R g loadings)	+0.037	**+ 0.080**	+0.088
WAIS-R to WAIS-III (WAIS-III g loadings)	+0.147	**+ 0.220**	+0.282
WAIS-III to WAIS-IV (WAIS-III g loadings)	+0.386	**+ 0.550**	+0.637
WAIS-III to WAIS-IV (WAIS-IV g loadings)	+0.315	**+ 0.672**	+0.575

In Table 2.2, I experiment to see what happens to correlations when coding gains are put at zero, so as to emphasize the absurdity of the significance of score gains on the subtests collectively being affected by performance on that one test (the least g loaded of the lot). Once again, Table A.7 gives all three values with the adjusted values in bold being those from Table 2.2.

In Table 2.3, I experimented to see what happens to correlations if we imagine US children being tutored so that they enjoyed something like the extra years of education adults enjoyed when more of them entered tertiary institutions. About half the difference between the WISC and WAIS correlations were eliminated. I will not offer what difference it makes to use method 2 for the adjusted values because it is clearly not worth the trouble.

CHAPTER 3

Dysgenics and Eugenics

The celebration of how environment has enhanced cognitive abilities omits something important about human progress. Environment and genes interact and the deterioration of genetic quality has the potential to do long-term harm. Just as natural selection produced a humanity with better genes for cognitive ability than the creatures from whom we evolved, there might be historical events or trends that indicate that hard-won ground is being lost.

Dysgenic trends are anything happening to the genes of the present generation that causes the next generation to have a lower IQ. Eugenics is the reverse. Hitler gave these terms a bad name because he used extermination and forced sterilization as his methods. His program was essentially: sterilization of the mentally retarded (inhumane but also unnecessary because they do not tend to overreproduce); the extermination of "non-Aryans" like Poles and Gypsies falsely thought to be inferior; and the extermination of other groups albeit on noneugenic grounds. Jews were not considered to have mentally inferior genes but were supposedly programmed to have personality traits that infected European culture. Communists and socialists were simply political opponents.

While I am not in sympathy with the assumptions of many who endorse eugenics, Hitler must be set aside. There is nothing intrinsically wrong with the goal of improving the genetic inheritance of the human race as far as cognitive abilities are concerned and methods must be judged on their merits.

3.1 POL POT AND CAMBODIA

Rulers can cause mass exterminations that have dysgenic effects no matter what their intent. Between 1973 and 1976, Pol Pot killed millions of Cambodians (Kampucheans). His criteria were purely political but discriminated to some degree against those with superior genes for IQ. He tried to eliminate urban dwellers (mildly superior because people abandon impoverished rural areas when they find they can be viable elsewhere) and anyone with "elite" qualifications (superior because access to education is to some degree competitive favoring those with greater talent). Those who wore spectacles were used as a criterion: they needed spectacles for a literate occupation and they had the money to afford them. He also destroyed all bicycles.

How much did Pol Pot do to lower the mean IQ of the Cambodian people? Sunic (2009) puts Croatians at a mean IQ of 90. He asks whether the communist massacre of hundreds of thousands of the Croat middle classes in 1945 was the answer. He accuses communists in general of "aristocide" in the sense that much killing, whatever the rationale, was motivated by hatred for those more successful and intelligent than oneself. He generalizes (p. 3/5) that communist aristicides have crippled the whole of Eastern Europe: "A large number of intelligent people were simply wiped out and could not pass their genes on to their offspring." None of these nations suffered massacres anything like the scale of Cambodia. It is hardly surprising that there has been public speculation about how much Cambodia's average IQ was reduced (Learning Diary, 2009).

This question can be settled by a few calculations. Pol Pot killed somewhere between 1.7 and 2.5 million people. I will put this at 2.1 million or 26% of Cambodia's 8 million people (Kiernan, 2002). If he had done it using IQ tests, eliminating the top 26% would have lowered the IQ of the remaining parents by 6.4 IQ points and a good portion of this deficit would have been handed down to their children. However, as we have seen, he in fact used occupation as his criterion.

We do not know the correlation between the occupational status of the parent and the IQ of their (no longer to be born) children, but in a semirural society it would be below that of the United States. At that time in the United States, it was 0.300 (Flynn, 2000b). If you eliminated the top 26% of the US population by occupation, the mean IQ of their children would drop by only 1.92 points. Moreover, Pol Pot did not really use a pure criterion of occupational status. For example, a lot of his henchmen doing the killing were intellectuals (Pol Pot attended the Sorbonne, although he did flunk all of his courses). When he tried to eliminate everyone who lived in the capital city of Phnom Penh, this included many in humble occupations. The genetic capital of the Cambodian people was lowered by not much more than an IQ point. The people were hardly stripped of intellectual talent.

Their recovery attests to this. Despite harassment by the remnants of Pol Pot's troops, the new Heng Samrin regime installed in 1979 did an almost incredible job of reconstruction. Faced with famine and no schools, books, hospitals, police, courts, civil service, mail, telephones, radio, or television, they educated a new administrative and technological elite and by 1985, the society had returned to normality (Flynn, 2012b).

Pol Pot provides not only an estimate of the quality of Cambodia's genes but also something more. He sets a probable limit on the dysgenic consequences of even the most horrific events of world history. Needless to say, the sins of totalitarianism should not be exonerated. Their consequences for rationality go far beyond the deterioration of genes. The Nazi elimination of the Jews decapitated the brains of its scientific establishment. It began to investigate the Nazi doctrine that the core of the earth was filled with ice: not some special kind of ice but just ordinary ice. In 1492, the expulsions of the Jews from Spain adversely affected its cognitive elite. However, whatever tyrants have done, they have never really lowered the human race's genetic capital for cognition.

Sunic (2009, p. 2/5) speculates about negative selection of genes for other behavioral traits: "Did communism ... give birth to a unique subspecies of people predisposed to communism?" For example, did it produce people who felt comfortable only with little personal freedom? I may be excused for not addressing that question.

3.2 REPRODUCTIVE PATTERNS

Setting the dramas of world history aside, there are those who fear that perfectly ordinary patterns of reproduction will, slowly but insidiously, lower genotypic IQ throughout the developed world. In recent years, Cattell, Murray and Herrnstein, and Lynn, among others, have emphasized dysgenic trends.

Raymond B. Cattell (1938, 1972, and 1987) is worth reading for the bizarre. He laments that we are breeding for pacifism and pleasure rather than pugnacity. Only warlike societies will transform humankind into a higher species. There should be no breeding across national lines, so that the societies that triumph shall not have their evolving genes diluted by others—like grasshoppers that diverge into species because they are isolated on mountaintops. The struggle for power need not decimate failed nations or races. They will be offered welfare if they agree not to reproduce. India was suspect because of it's lack of a Calvinist ethic and blacks were hopeless. Lack of intellect, despite charming characteristics like humor and religiosity, dictate confinement on nonreproductive reservations (toned down after the 1930s). It would be no bad thing if a nuclear war subjected a literate residue to high mutation rates: these speed up genetic novelties. Outer space sends no communications because all alien species have opted for the general happiness, a miserable thing with no evolutionary potential (Flynn, 2000a).

Lynn, on the other hand, captures every facet of a serious case for the deterioration of our genes. *Dysgenics* (1996) sets 1850 as the year in which advanced societies saw eugenic reproductive trends turn into dysgenic trends.

Prior to that time, the upper classes were more efficient at passing their genes on to the next generation. They had the means to give their children a better chance of surviving until adulthood, while the children of the lower classes tended to be decimated by poverty, disease, and relative neglect. The latter often abandoned their newborn children to die. After 1850, public health, growing prosperity, and the welfare state, including the eventual support of mothers who had been abandoned by their partners, favored the children of the lower classes and tended to equalize survival rates. Equally important, those who were more intelligent, better educated, and more self-controlled began to use contraception, so that their counterparts in the lower classes who failed to use it began to have higher fertility rates. Modern schooling increased the correlation of class with IQ. Graduates had fewer children than dropouts. The result was that each generation began to show low-IQ people handing on their genes more efficiently than those with high IQs (Lynn, 1996, chaps. 2 and 3).

3.2.1 The Multiplication of the "Scum-Worthy"

The interesting thing is not only the consequences that were anticipated but also how they were characterized. Darwin was a thoroughly good man and I have no desire to make him seem blameworthy by taking him out of historical context. But, at times at least, he reflected the prejudices of his day regarding human beings at the bottom of the social scale.

Darwin (1871, p. 510) lamented that physicians prolong the lives of everyone and as a result, " ... weak members of civilized societies propagate their kind. No-one will doubt that this must be highly injurious to the race of man." The man who also independently discovered the theory of natural selection, Alfred Russell Wallace, records a conversation between the two men (1890, p. 93): Darwin is oppressed by the tendency of "the lower classes" to overreproduce and characterizes the surplus as children of "the scum." Wallace's memory could be at fault. However, by 1890, Wallace had totally rejected this image of "civilized society." He was adamant that English society was too corrupt and unjust to allow any reasonable determination of who was fit or unfit. He respected Darwin and was unlikely to so describe his views without foundation.

Spencer (1874, p. 286) lamented "aid to the bad" as hindering society in its efforts to eliminate "good for nothings." William Graham Sumner calls them shiftless, worthless, and pretty much anything else he could think of (Flynn, 2000a). All three castigated the nascent welfare state of their time and in addition, Sumner led a crusade against any private charity that aided the unfit.

The fear of the scum perpetuating itself is based on the assumption that the scum of one generation have something about them, something that ensures that their children will be the scum of the next generation. In 1870, the elite were not aware of the modern word "gene," but there is no doubt that they believed that a large number of people had heritable traits that put them beyond salvation. Although no one would be impolite enough to use the word "scum" today, the thesis is very much alive: the notion that the genes of a substantial part of society mean that their IQ and other personal traits, such as resistance to education, welfare dependency, and criminality, are fixed at a particular time and not subject to modification by new social conditions.

For shorthand (and rhetoric) I will call this thesis by its original name: a large number of people are "scum-worthy." Those who wish can substitute "elimination-worthy." Surely that is the cash value of "we want to eliminate your genes because you are likely to have children like yourselves." Whatever the phrase, it assumes that our minds and characters are "frozen." History has proven that it is mistaken. Some years ago, I noted that the percentage of black women who suffer from solo parenthood fluctuates as the percentage of black men who are viable spouses varies. Fewer of the latter, the more black women find husbands; more of the latter, the fewer black women find husbands and the more they become solo mothers (Flynn, 2008).

I reject the thesis of "scum today, scum tomorrow." If you have a fixed pool of "scum," and take their IQ at a given time as a badge of their inferiority, then if IQ falls from one generation to another, the percentage of scum increases. On the other hand, if the lower classes can be drained of scum from one generation to another, if they are not permanently scum-worthy, society may cause a net loss of low-IQ people and/or undesirable personal traits. The whole drift of this book is how the development of modernity altered the minds and capacities of people over time.

3.2.2 America and Britain

Using UK data, Lynn (2011, pp. 104) estimates a loss of 4.4 IQ points between 1890 and 1980 in terms of the quality of genes for intelligence. For white Americans, he posits a decline at 5.0 points between 1885 and 2010 (Lynn, 2011, p. 130). Well if so, the genetic decline did not add to the scum. During that period, the average IQ rose by 30 points and the mass of people that the elite wrote off, actually became the population of the modern world. While IQ gains in most nations have tended to be uniform over the whole IQ scale, those at the bottom have made, if anything, slightly larger gains. Many of the lower classes became the people we see around us today: capable of education, staffing all of the important social roles once thought the prerogatives of the upper class, and less violent by far than the people of 1850 (see the next chapter), and so forth.

Lynn, it should be said, tries to stipulate carefully who should not be allowed to reproduce, rather than making a blanket accusation versus the lower classes. Charles Murray believes, as most of us do, that Americans in general deserve a valued place in society appreciated by relatives and associates. But the substance of frozen minds appears in Murray (cited by Lynn). He provides a table in which we are told that, other things being equal, a loss of three IQ points over this generation will mean that the number of women chronically dependent on welfare will increase by 7%; illegitimacy by 8%; men interned in jail by 12%; and the number of permanent high school dropouts by nearly 15% (Herrnstein and Murray, 1994).

Now both Lynn and Herrnstein and Murray refer to the "Flynn Effect" (Murray coined the term). When Murray says that social statistics will deteriorate "all things being equal," he may include the fact that IQ gains over time have ceased. But they never fully acknowledge that the malleability of people's IQ and traits shows how wildly premature the predictions of the eugenicists turned out to be. Lynn makes the point that the fact that the soil (the environment) is continually enriched does not make insignificant the fact that the seed (genes) have deteriorated. Fair enough, particularly if IQ gains stop. But it turned out that the soil was so barren it could be enormously enriched and could overwhelm any genetic deterioration for at least 150 years.

3.2.3 International Data
Lynn (1996, pp. 99, 117, 118, and 133) finds that the decline of genetic IQ was replicated within the United Kingdom in England, Scotland, and Northern Ireland, also in Ireland, Australia, and Canada, and in many nations of continental Europe. There were two exceptions.

In Sweden, *circa* 1970, data on the IQs of parents and the number of their children still living at home was collected for 1746 residents of the county of Stockholm, excluding the city itself (Lynn, 1996, p. 98). Taking parents aged 26–45, almost all of whose children were still living at home, the pattern is mildly eugenic. Parents at IQs of 95 and above have 1.7 children compared to those 94 and below who have 1.6 children. Older parents aged 46–65 show virtually the same pattern. Concerning this age group, Lynn points out that the children who had left home would have been more prominent in low-IQ families in that they typically leave home to have their own children at earlier ages. However, as for children unmarried, there is an equal case that high-IQ families had more self-achieving children who were away from home pursuing higher education or holding jobs. As Lynn says, this sample was mainly suburban and it would be better to have data from rural areas. He notes that rural residents tend to have lower IQs and may have higher birth rates. This does not count. Put their mean at 95: if those above that mean tend to have slightly more children than those below, rural areas would still show a mildly eugenic tendency.

The parents in this study would have been born between 1905 and 1944. Lynn (2011, p. 181) cites a recent study done on Swedish men and women born from 1945 to 1950 classed by socioeconomic status (SES). With the data on fathers and mothers merged, the number of offspring above and below the mean is identical, with a very slight eugenic bias thanks to a few more children at the top. All in all, Sweden qualifies as eugenic/dysgenic neutral.

Lynn (1996, p. 133; 2011, p. 181) includes Norway in a table that gives the number of children per parent classed by SES. The dysgenic ratios he gives for each nation in this table (and throughout the book) should be discarded. For example, he puts the dysgenic ratio for Norwegian parents born between 1885 and 1900 at 1.60. This is simply dividing the lowest class or class 5 (6.07 children per adult) by class 1 (3.80) with no regard as to what the ratios are for other classes above and below the SES mean. Without an estimate of the size of the classes and the IQ mean for each, it is not possible to get a true dysgenic ratio. But assuming each class is of equal size, we can take each value and divide by the total giving us the percentage of each class in the new generation. We can then subtract those below the middle class from those above it and get how many births out of a hundred are below-average births uncompensated by above-average births. The number for this population is 11.01, which I will call the negative deficit.

The corrected Norwegian data are fascinating. Four sets of parents ranging from those born 1885–1890 to those born 1925–1930 show the negative deficit going from 11.01 to 12.14 to 10.42 to 0.39 or essentially nil (0.39 births uncompensated out of 100). This last would be a loss of about 0.10 IQ points between the generations.

Sundet, Borren, and Tambs (2008) have updated Norwegian trends from massive data sets. For many years, the military gave virtually all males (95%) a battery of tests at the age of 19. These were similar to Raven's plus the Wechsler Arithmetic and Similarities subtests. From these, they calculated an overall IQ score for 100,000 men born between 1950 and 1965. In 2000 (when the men were aged 35–52) they matched them with their names in Norwegian census data to determine their number of offspring. They found that the correlation between father's IQ and number of children was mildly positive (eugenic) at 0.02. The census also had the father's educational level. They were classified as high, moderate, and low and these levels were correlated with their number of children. Interestingly, the correlations were negative 0.16 for fathers born *circa* 1950. However, they fell to a negligible negative of 0.05 as we approach fathers born in 1965.

There is a final piece of data that indicates when Norway's dysgenic trends disappeared. Draftees tested from 1957 to 1959 were 19 years old at that time, and their parents would have been born a generation earlier from about 1913 to 1915. Therefore, they provide an insight into reproductive patterns a century ago. When ranked by IQ level of the draftee and the number of their siblings counted, there was a negative correlation of about 0.20. This confirms Lynn's data that parents born before 1925 did indeed have a dysgenic mating pattern. Draftees tested from 1969 to 2002, whose parents were born from 1925 to 1958, show a steady decline to a small negative correlation of 0.045. The year 1958 falls midway between 1950 and 1965, the period during which our best data indicates a transition to mildly positive eugenic trends. All in all, Norway joins Sweden as a nation that today shows no significant dysgenic trend.

The fact that these nations are exceptions links three themes: the persistence of IQ gains, the persistence of dysgenic reproductive trends, and the consequences of the welfare state. Scandinavia is important because it appears that IQ gains have ended there. Therefore, if dysgenic reproductive trends by class persisted in those states, there would be no Flynn Effect to offset them. But they have not persisted. This prompts a reassessment of the fact that those who lament dysgenic trends also attack the welfare state. They never drive the indictment home by the simplest of methods: rank all developed nations according to the maturity of their welfare state; rank them all according to their dysgenic trends; and show that two hierarchies coincide.

Sweden and Norway would stand at the top of the welfare state hierarchy. Therefore, such an analysis would falsify their thesis. The use of the welfare state and other progressive measures in Scandinavia has created a relatively egalitarian or classless society. Recall that their egalitarian societies were credited with halting IQ gains (good schooling and quality of life for all, optimum parenting and ratio of adults to children in homes for all, occupations that had fully exploited the trend toward more elite occupations, and here we must add equal use of contraception by all). These same attributes now seem to have forestalled dysgenic reproductive differences between the classes. In sum, by happy chance, egalitarian policies have ended both IQ gains and dysgenic trends at the same time. So there is no need for the former to offset the latter!

3.2.4 The Welfare Stare

The notion of the abolition of the welfare state as a method of ending dysgenic reproduction raises a question. At one time, it was believed correctly that without the welfare state some significant percentage of solo mothers and their children would die and rectify the situation. But today, no one wants to go back to mothers abandoning newborn children on trash heaps. Herrnstein and Murray (1994, pp. 544–549) endorse two proposals: an end to government programs for all women who have babies, whether they are married or not; and that unmarried mothers shall have no legal basis to demand that the father provide child support.

They argue that the first will reduce the incentive for poor mothers to have children. This is debatable: throughout the world, the more poor people, the more children, even when faced with economic want. In New Zealand, the child benefit, and capitalizing on it to buy a home, encouraged many in the main stream of society to have an extra child. Given over population, it may be worth setting a limit to the number of offspring any person can have throughout their life without forfeiting the child to foster care. But that is another question and fraught with difficulty. The second proposal can only make males more ready to father children out of wedlock: they will pay no penalty unless you now threaten them with jail. It may be said that abolishing the welfare state will eventually improve the lot of the poor by ending welfare dependency and getting them into remunerative work. I cannot discuss this larger economic debate here. But I await such a society that presents an example of a disappearing "underclass," one whose absence shames those that have resorted to the welfare state.

Sweden and Norway signal why I answered as I did when asked, "how could New Zealand abolish dysgenic reproduction between the classes." I said eliminate poverty and create an egalitarian society.

When asked, "was that likely in New Zealand or most of Europe?" I had to say no. And when asked, "could I guarantee that IQ gains would persist in most developed nations?" I said that I could not. Who knows what demands the societies of the future will make on the cognitive abilities of their people? The upper classes may be susceptible to the idle corruption that afflicted the elite in Rome. Progress in curing the ills of the lower classes may cease.

So does the future hold out any hope (other than the Scandinavian option)? All of us value the contributions of an ever-more intelligent society: truth, beauty, and goodness. The prospect of deteriorating genes for IQ, century after century, cannot appeal even when environment compensates.

3.2.5 The New Eugenics

Taking the traditional reproductive pattern between the classes in most advanced nations, there is no need to panic. Lynn (2011, pp. 99, 102, 103) uses fertility data to put the current dysgenic trend in the United States and the United Kingdom at a loss of 0.80 IQ points per generation. He rightly observes that this estimate does not distinguish genetic effects from environmental effects and therefore, multiplies the value by 0.71 (his estimate of heritability narrow). So 0.80 times 0.71 equals 0.57 IQ points of genetic decline. Over 100 years (3.33 generations), this would amount to less than two IQ points. What might occur over the next century to offset this, that is, modify the fact that the lower classes have more children than the upper classes?

In *Eugenics: A reassessment* (2001), Lynn sees some hopeful new trends in what he calls the new eugenics. This has two prongs: universal contraception among all classes; and use of modern techniques to upgrade the quality of the offspring that are created and not aborted.

I can see no objection to steps that would give lower class and demoralized women more control over their fertility. They aspire to no more offspring than any other class (Lynn, 2001, p. 166). However, take the example of the pill. If you are well organized, you obtain it and take it every day. If you are demoralized, you may be remiss and have intercourse without its protection. Indeed, you may be ill-informed about the merits of different contraceptive devices (particularly the morning-after pill). America is far behind Western Europe in general sophistication about contraception. Finally, you are more likely to be at the mercy of physicians who are reluctant to arrange abortions.

Lynn makes an interesting suggestion: imagine that at puberty all women were made immune to conception and had to take steps to become pregnant. The fact that one had to plan one's pregnancy would suddenly favor those capable of planning over those who were not. Thus, the lower class bias toward unplanned pregnancy would be transformed overnight toward an upper class bias toward planned pregnancy. As Lynn points out, there is already the Norplant II pill that can be inserted under the skin and ban pregnancy for 5 years. At any time, it can be removed and the flow of progestin (caused by the pill) stopped. At the end of 5 years, it can be renewed. Who knows what science will do in inventing a safe contraceptive that could render all women (or men) temporarily infertile from puberty?

What might motivate the "inoculation" of all children against pregnancy? This is unpredictable but the falling age of puberty is a possibility. If the 11-year-old children of the middle classes come home pregnant or having fathered a child, that might be an incentive. Ideally, all children would be inoculated just as they are against childhood diseases. Failing that, contraceptive devices and counseling should be made more available to all. Apparently barbers are used in continental Europe. But there could be a subprofessional who dispenses advice and contraception stationed adjacent to every American supermarket, or any shop where women are likely to appear.

Most of all, Lynn relies on upgrading the offspring that are created and not aborted. As for abortion, there is prenatal diagnosis of genetic diseases and disorders plus fetuses with Down's syndrome, and these are near universally available. As for upgrading the offspring, there is artificial insemination by selected donors, *in vitro* fertilization and implantation, with genetic engineering and cloning in the wings. It would be better if these techniques were available to all but in many societies they may be fee for service and used by say the upper 80%. Even this, would mean that most parents would elect to have children dominated by genes that were more intelligent and healthy. Cattell's dream of an upgraded species may occur without his incredible scenario.

Lynn predicts that totalitarian regimes will use the new eugenics more effectively than democracies (as when Eastern Europe engineered elite athletes for the Olympics). They will also use sterilization to pre-vent those with heritable disorders, sociopaths, recidivist criminals, and those with Down's syndrome, from reproducing. However, their main advantage, as we shall see, is that they will control immigration. Against this, I will add that there is a darker side to the record of total-itarian states and the human intellect.

3.3 RACE AND IMMIGRATION

Thus far we have treated the American and European class structure as static: as if the population were self-contained and expanded only by indigenous natural increase.

Lynn (2001) discusses the effects of immigration, a factor in virtu-ally every European nation. Some nations control immigration by accepting mainly those who have skills to contribute that are scarce. The European Union has the problem of migration across one another's borders and the United States has the problem of clandestine immigration over its Mexican border. You may wonder why this is never controlled no matter who rules, Democrat or Republican. It is because much of American business, particularly agribusiness, and the middle class want low-paid workers and servants. Thus, despite all the hue and cry, the will is lacking. The United States will have to make up its mind: does it need the cheap labor enough to compensate for whatever social problems the immigrants cause?

In the second edition of *Dysgenics* (2011, pp. 267, 269, 270), Lynn raises his estimate of dysgenic trends in America and Britain. Thanks to immigration and natural increase that favors Hispanics and blacks, the United States will lose fully 4.4 IQ points (3.1 points genetic IQ) between 2000 and 2050. By 2050, census data indicate that Hispanics and blacks will be 45% of the population. Britain will decline by 2.5 IQ points (1.8 points genetic IQ) between 2006 and 2056 thanks to a population 27% of whom are largely South Asians and Africans from the Caribbean and sub-Saharan Africa. He argues that all of these races have genes for IQ that limit their potential to match Europeans. This is an issue so complex that it would be fruitless to debate it in a few words. I refer the reader to works in which I argue that East Asians, whites, and blacks probably have roughly equivalent genes for

IQ (Flynn, 1980, 1991, 2008, 2012a). Here I will refer only to data (some of it new) that are highly relevant.

First, it is true that most developing nations have contemporary IQs ranging from 70 to 90. Their immigration to European nations throughout the world will lower mean IQ therein. However, many of them are in the earliest stage of industrialization. Moreover, what of the United States and Britain? They both had average IQs of 70 as of 1900, when Britain had behind it at least 50 years of industrialization (from 1850) and America at least 35 years (from the end of the Civil War). We have data about rising IQ and industrialization going hand in hand in several nations, for example, Turkey, Kenya, and Brazil (Flynn, 2012a). Does the third world really have worse genes for IQ?

Second, Lynn (1987) has proposed an evolutionary scenario that ranks the races into a genetic hierarchy. He hypothesizes that extreme cold created a more challenging environment. During the Ice Ages, the ancestors of East Asians are supposed to have been north of the Himalayas where the cold was most intense, the ancestors of whites north of the Alps where the cold was next worst, and the ancestors of blacks still in Africa where it was relatively warm. Therefore, we have a hierarchy of running from East Asians to whites to blacks.

This evolutionary scenario is false (Flynn, 2012a). China's population is a blend of two groups that had very different locations during the Ice Ages. The Han Chinese people may have been north of the Himalayas in an area of extreme cold. The "quasi-Malay" Chinese of the south took the coastal route out of Africa to China, along the Arabian coast, through India, and eventually through Southeast Asia. They never suffered from extreme cold. The two groups met at modern Shanghai or along the Yangtze River. Since then, Han genes have slowly spread downward from the north. Nonetheless, as you go from the north toward the southeast provinces, the balance between Han genes and "coastal" genes begins to shift toward the latter with the greatest concentration in Guangdong Province (Chen et al., 2009).

The DNA of the Chinese of Singapore shows that they are overwhelmingly from Guangdong. Lynn and Vanhanen (2006) put Singapore at top of the world with a mean IQ of 108. If one isolates the 74% of Singapore's people that are Chinese, their mean rises to 114. Mainland China gets only 105.

The Singapore high score may make the reader suspect that whatever the cause, Chinese have superior genes for intelligence. If so, see Flynn (1991, 2009, pp. 115–122). I should add that Singapore has the advantage of a highly urbanized environment and its IQ estimate may be deceptively high. It would be wrong to assume that not being north of the Himalayas conferred a genetic advantage on the South Chinese.

There is a Chinese web site that invites people to take a 60-item IQ test based on the Stanford–Binet and classifies their scores by province (IQED.com.cn). They have averaged the results of over 63,000 IQs. What these offer is interesting but must, of course, be validated by careful sampling. You must be alert to the fact that they call all members of the dominant group in China "Han." They use this as an ethic category, inclusive of those with Han culture and "Han genes" plus those with Han culture and "coastal genes." It merely means Chinese as distinct from non-Chinese minorities.

Setting aside provinces with significant non-Chinese minorities, the remaining 20 provinces are represented by subjects that number from 1070 to 6635, with the exception of the northern province of Gansu at 605. The provincial averages are remarkably uniform. The overall average is 105.60 with a variation by province from 103 to 107; only highly urbanized Shanghai stands at 108. The six southern provinces (at 105.50) and the 11 northern provinces (at 105.27) are virtually identical. There are three provinces in the middle that are about 1.5 points higher (thanks to including Shanghai). Guangdong Province has 5510 subjects and a mean of 106. This score in not inflated by Hong Kong for which there are no data.

You can always try to patch up the Ice Ages hypothesis by arguing that the South Chinese were just as highly selected for intelligence as the North Chinese. You need a substitute for the absence of extreme cold, for example, introducing some other factor that had exactly the same effect. Perhaps they profited from "the Malthusian carry-load," which is to say that their poverty was so great that only the brightest survived (Unz, 1981). This new evolutionary theory will no doubt spread despite all that needs to be shown to give it any credibility. Did the North Chinese suffer from less poverty? Otherwise they had a double advantage. What about sub-Saharan Africa where poverty has been endemic over the last 500 years? Are they forging ahead of Europeans? What of India? Maybe abject poverty promotes the survival of the most brutal, or forbids large human communities with a social structure in which brightness prevails.

Give me any difference concerning group performance and I will find a remote evolutionary scenario to explain it. What is important are current evolutionary trends. As Lynn says, before contraception, the well-off had more means to ensure the survival of their children. Now that we have the new eugenics, and something approaching universal contraception, affluence may once again encourage the survival of the brightest.

3.3.1 Immigration Reconsidered

No matter who is correct about the genetic capital of immigrants, they will certainly have lower IQs than the people they join for some generations. Lynn goes beyond this. He assumes that when they arrive they have a gravitational effect that pulls the nation's whole IQ curve downward, for example, even those with elite IQs are somehow diminished. For those of you who are specialists, he does this by using the table of values under a normal curve. He treats the original population plus the immigrants as a merged population with the same IQ variance they had before. In fact, when you add a low-IQ group to the bottom of a higher IQ group the variance of the resulting population is increased. But the point can be made in ordinary language.

Imagine you pulled the island of Dominica northward so that it now had a common border with Florida. Adding it to the United States would, by definition, lower the newly created average IQ. But it would also stretch the range of IQs downward. Which is to say, it would leave the original inhabitants of the United States untouched. Whatever genetic capital these people had the day before would remain the day after. The elite with IQs above 130 (the top 2.27%) would still be there to run society. If immigration added 10% to the population, the elite percentage would fall slightly: 2.27 divided by 110 equals 2.06%. But their absolute number would be unchanged. There would be some intermarriage, of course. However, the US elite do not tend to marry their servants or the people who pick their grapes. They tend to marry people with matching IQs, which would include only the very elite among the immigrants, and this would do the next generation of the elite no harm at all.

This brings us back to the question of a balance sheet for accepting unskilled immigrants: will cheap labor or the problems of unassimilated ethnic groups do more to promote or retard economic growth and the quality of life? It is true that unassimilated immigrants may be more resistant to the new eugenics, the trends that may tend to eliminate dysgenic reproductive trends among the classes. They themselves will be divided into classes. If the lower class within their community uses contraception less often than their more educated classes, there will be a mild dysgenic tendency. I doubt that this will count for much against the pros and cons of the economic debate.

3.3.2 Geopolitical Consequences

Lynn (2011) notes that across the world, nations with lower IQs are having more children than nations with higher IQs. This will lower the world's average IQ. But it is a dysgenic tendency only if you concede that nations with lower IQs cannot rival whites because of their genes.

He believes that worldwide dysgenic trends will alter the relative power of nations. Unlike democratic nations, the totalitarian state of China will bar immigration by other races (recall that he considers Chinese to be at the top of the genetic hierarchy) and will systemically promote the new eugenics. The United States will be weakened most of all, partially by leaving the new eugenics to private initiative but mainly because of massive immigration. White versus black versus Hispanic antagonism may divide America into three states and even if not, the resulting internal conflict will be crippling. Thanks to her growing advantage in terms of genetic capital, China will dominate the world economically and militarily. He does not discuss a darker side of totalitarianism (although he does mention it elsewhere). It tends to kill, imprison, and exile its best minds and fetter the free debate that remedies corruption and incompetence.

Without conceding Lynn's contentions, Chinese dominance might happen anyway. Therefore, it is worth assessing his scenario. He believes that China will pacify the entire world as part of her realm. Wonderful if it were true. She would have done something America cannot do, despite enormous predominance since 1946. He believes that China will rule the world piecemeal: they will appoint governors for every nation including the United States. What possible purpose

China would have in trying to govern the Congo, Somalia, the Middle East, and so forth is left unclear. As for sending troops everywhere to create "un-failed" states, America's recent history of bleeding itself white to do so might be a deterrent. I presume that China does not believe it has a magic formula to keep Sunnis and Shiites from each other's throats. As for ruling the United States, I believe she might be inhibited from trying to govern it because Americans can hardly govern it themselves.

I think that what China would want from the rest of the world is what she has got at present. Trading partners sufficiently healthy to be sources of foreign exchange and investment (you do not kill trading partners, you nurture them) and allowing the Third World to find its way if it can. If it worries about its security, it can tell everyone else to divest itself of nuclear weapons and inspect them, and then use drones and infiltration against any terrorists that pose a threat to China. In other words, what China would like to do then is pretty much what America would like to do now. Positing that it will have a totalitarian government endlessly into the future reminds one about predictions about the USSR. The prediction neglects whether China, without political change, can satisfy the aspirations of the rural poor and withstand the growing hilarity of educated urbanites about how silly the antics of its leadership strike them (Flynn, 2010).

Setting aside the effects of what great power dominates the world, Americans would not like to lose that role to China. They would not like to disintegrate into three nations. The hypothesis that differential migration and totalitarianism play key roles rests on three premises: blacks and Hispanics, really Hispanics, have genes for intelligence that rank them below non-Hispanic whites; China will remain a totalitarian state; and totalitarian states will apply the new eugenics with much greater effect. I doubt the first and am agnostic about the second. As for the third, I have not forgotten what totalitarianism does to deaden the intellect. I suspect its record in this regard will offset whatever extra gains it gets from the new eugenics.

3.4 SUMMARY

If you want to abolish dysgenic reproduction, advanced nations should follow Sweden and Norway: abolish poverty so the lower classes will have middle class aspirations and knowledge of contraception. Even where this is not done, as in the United States and United Kingdom, the rate among the native population is slow enough to tolerate for a century, particularly if the Flynn Effect persists. Even if it does not, those nations may raise their average genetic IQ by using the new eugenic techniques. Immigration is a long-term problem only if you believe that black and Hispanic genes limit their potential. Even if you have a mild leaning in that direction, industrial society creates unskilled work the native population is unwilling to do. The rationale for many immigrants is that they will do it and thereby promote economic growth.

China, assuming its stability and ascendancy, is not going to meddle with the internal politics of other states more than the United States has done—probably it will do less. Eugenics/dysgenics does not supply a theory of history that decides whether the souls of America and Europe are to be saved or damned. It is an analysis of one trend, probably not a very important trend, among all those that will determine the course of the next century. As the next chapter will show, I am far more concerned about things like climate change and whether the world can be pacified without being merged into one state.

REFERENCES

Cattell, R. B. (1938). *Psychology and the religious quest*. London: Thomas Nelson.

Cattell, R. B. (1972). *A new morality from science: Beyondism*. Elmsford, NY: Pergamon.

Cattell, R. B. (1987). *Beyondism: Religion from science*. New York, NY: Praeger.

Chen, J., Zheng, H., Bei, J. -X., Sun, L., Jia, W. -H., Li, T., et al. (2009). Genetic structure of the Han Chinese population revealed by genome-wide SNP variation. *The American Journal of Human Genetics, 85*, 775–785.

Darwin, C. (1871). *The descent of man and selection in relation to sex*. London: MacMillan.

Flynn, J. R. (1980). *Race, IQ, and Jensen*. London: Routledge.

Flynn, J. R. (1991). *Asian Americans: Achievement beyond IQ*. Hillsdale, NJ: Erlbaum.

Flynn, J. R. (2000a). *How to defend humane ideals: Substitutes for objectivity*. Lincoln, NB: University of Nebraska Press.

Flynn, J. R. (2000b). IQ trends over time: Intelligence, race, and meritocracy. In K. Arrow, S. Bowles, & S. Durlauf (Eds.), *Meritocracy and economic inequality* (pp. 35–60). Princeton, NJ: Princeton University Press.

Flynn, J. R. (2008). *Where have all the liberals gone? Race, class, and ideals in America*. Cambridge UK: Cambridge University Press.

Flynn, J. R. (2009). *What is intelligence? Beyond the flynn effect*. Cambridge UK: Cambridge University Press [Expanded paperback edition].

Flynn, J. R. (2010). *The torchlight list: Around the world in 200 books*. Wellington, New Zealand: AWA Press.

Flynn, J. R. (2012a). *Are we getting smarter: Rising IQ in the twenty-first century*. Cambridge UK: Cambridge University Press.

Flynn, J. R. (2012b). *Beyond patriotism: From Truman to Obama*. Exeter, UK: Imprint Academic.

Herrnstein, R. J., & Murray, C. (1994). *The bell curve: Intelligence and class structure in American life*. New York, NY: The Free Press.

Kiernan, B. (2002). *The Pol Pot regime: Race, power and genocide in Cambodia under the Khmer Rouge, 1975–1979*. New Haven, CT: Yale University Press.

Learning Diary. (2009). The learning diary of an Israeli water engineer: Aristicide in Cambodia? Accessed 11.05.2009.

Lynn, R. (1987). The intelligence of Mongoloids: A psychometric, evolutionary, and neurological theory. *Personality and Individual Differences, 8*, 813–844.

Lynn, R. (1996). *Dysgenics: Genetic deterioration in modern populations*. Westport, CT: Praeger.

Lynn, R. (2001). *Eugenics: A reassessment*. Westport, CT: Praeger.

Lynn, R., & Vanhanen, T. (2006). *IQ and global inequality*. Augusta, GA: Washington Summit Publishers.

Lynn, R. (2011). *Dysgenics: Genetic deterioration in modern populations* (2nd ed.). Belfast: Ulster Institute for Social Research.

Spencer, H. (1874). *Study of sociology*. London: MacMillan.

Sundet, J. M., Borren, I., & Tambs, K. (2008). The Flynn effect is partly caused by changing fertility patters. *Intelligence, 36*, 183–191.

Sunic, T. (2009). *Dysgenics of a Communistkilling field: The Croatian Bleiburg*. Brussels Belgium: European Action.

Unz, R. (1981). *Preliminary notes on the possible sociobiological implications of the rural Chinese economy*. Cambridge MA: Harvard (unpublished manuscript). <www.ronunz.org/wp-content/uploads/2012/05/ChineseIntelligence.pd> Accessed 28.02.13.

Wallace, A. R. (1890). Human selection. *Popular Science Monthly, 38*, 90–102.

CHAPTER 4

Genes and Moral Progress

We leave behind the quality of our genes over the next century for a narrative that spans thousands of years. As a species, our evolutionary origins selected for aggressive genes particularly in males. But the trend toward larger and larger communities has domesticated our genes toward self-restraint and nonviolence and hence, improved character. For much of recent history, morality has been rule-bound with a content dictated partially by superstition and cruel commandments. But the trend toward rationality has replaced rules with principles ever more inclusive and humane. Because character plus principles is what morality is all about, I will call this moral progress.

Anthropologists dislike talk about progress because they assume the equal integrity of all cultures, which is contravened by ranking them in a hierarchy from lower to higher. To assess cultures means making a value judgment independent of the task of understanding them and appreciating what they mean to those who people them. I am not using "progress" to make a supracultural claim that ours is better than others or the present better than the past or the here better than the there. But I am claiming what is manifest: thanks to science we are epistemologically better off. We know far more about the real world than prescientific cultures do. And I am claiming that our behavior and principles are more humane than in the past. I think humane ideals can be justified (Flynn, 2000) but let that pass. Anyone is free to classify my value judgments as arbitrary, so long as they concede that rationality and humanity are our best hope of living through the remainder of this century without events we would find unwelcome.

4.1 OUR GENETIC INHERITANCE

Our nearest primate relatives suggest that over much of human evolution, males and females were subject to different selective pressures:

1. Males competed for access to females by either violent combat or aggressive displays that intimidated rivals. As aggressive males fathered the most offspring, their genes became dominant.

2. Females perpetuated their genes to the extent that they raised their children to maturity, so that their children could reproduce. A bond with a male helpmate was advantageous. Therefore, genes for whatever helped domesticate males were positively selected. These proclivities prepared the way for the emergence of traits that statistically differentiate the genders. It is politically incorrect to assert that women are cleaner, more attentive to physical appearance, more skilled at arts that make home life attractive, and more likely to use charm rather than (overtly) aggressively behavior to attract the opposite sex. I will rely on those of both sexes who see through their eyes and not their ideologies.

4.1.1 The Long-Term Domestication of Our Genes

Hallpike (2008) points out that male aggression may well have begun to pay decreased procreative dividends even in the simplest Homo sapiens societies, the hunter–gatherer societies that were universal until about 10,000 years ago. The simple societies that survive today show that an overly aggressive male can be eliminated or expelled by the collective action of other males and that the best hunter is expected to share his kill (after all, spoilage makes most of it worthless to him) just like anyone else. This is not to say violence about access to women was nonexistent, particularly in societies where female infanticide created a surplus of males.

About 10,000 years ago, thanks to agriculture, human beings started living in settled dwellings and larger communities, which were functional only if aggression was restricted by rules. Just as they had domesticated animals like dogs and cats, people began to domesticate themselves. Just as domesticated animals were selected for self-control of their aggressive behavior, not to be directed at their masters but to be governed by rules the master set, so people were domesticated by genetic selection for self-control and rule-bound behavior. Two of my colleagues have been seminal thinkers in this area. In *Domestication of the human species* (1988), Peter Wilson went so far as to argue that human vision was affected by the growing need to read the faces of others, thus to assess their moods and intentions. Helen Leach (2003) has analyzed the parallels between domesticated animals and increasingly domesticated humans.

She notes that the social domestication of humans is widely accepted but wishes to make a case for biological domestication. Anthropologists actually use certain morphological changes in skeletons as evidence that an animal species was being domesticated. These include craniofacial shortening and reductions in the robustness of the skeleton, tooth size, and overall size. She points to similar changes in some human populations starting as early as the late Pleistocene era, and invokes unconscious selection of genes as explanations of both trends.

The similarity between the physical changes of human beings and their domesticated animals is much debated. Brüne (2007) concludes that the parallels are not exact and that the human processes should be called "domestication-like." Be that as it may, sharing kills, bartering produce, mutually beneficial exchanges between producers and consumers or artisans and customers, sedentary residence in communities with increasingly effective central regulation, and above all, competition for women focused on money, status, and amiability (a nice guy), all of this should have moderated aggressive genes to some degree.

Let me put the point in evolutionary terms: assume that over 1000 generations law-abiding citizens have out-reproduced those predisposed to violence. If so, human genes were selected so that we find it easier today to live together without physical aggression. This is plausible but of course unproven. At a minimum we can say this: even if human genes have not been tamed, our original primate inheritance allowed for modification of aggressive behavior far more than its origins suggest.

4.1.2 The Short-Term Domestication of Males

Males are responsible for most acts of violence. The domestication of males by females is signaled by the fact that males are violent primarily between puberty and sometime in the 20s, after which they are pacified by the responsibilities of marriage and child rearing (Pinker, 2011). Violence has dropped over time as women achieved the equality that empowers them versus males in the home: the ability to find employment so that they need not be totally dependent on males to support themselves and their children, the presumption that both sexes will contribute to home maintenance and child rearing, the fact that division of property and child support means that a male cannot evade responsibilities through divorce, and legal sanctions against domestic violence.

While domestic violence is primarily a male tactic to assert control over women in the home, it is not without risk. Women sometimes settle disputes in their own favor. Menninger (1938, p. 183) reports a case in which a wife beat her husband to death with a hammer, locked their apartment, and then drove 50 miles to a bridge party.

Sunni Muslims interpret Islamic law (Shari law) as allowing a man to divorce his wife simply by saying "I divorce thee" three times. The husband is no longer responsible for the wife's expenses (but is responsible for the maintenance of children until they are weaned). The Cairo trilogy of Naguib Mahfouz (1956, 1957a, 1957b) illustrates the effects of the powerlessness of women in terms of domesticating male behavior. The husbands simply spend their evenings as they like: gambling, sexual adventure, and drink. Wives have no choice but to accept these as male prerogatives. A wife who rebelled against her husband bringing a prostitute into her home was simply discarded.

Enhanced power has changed the division of responsibilities that wives negotiate with their husbands. Few today would internalize the attitude of Nabokov's (author of *Lolita*) wife who construed her role as adoration. She attended all of his lectures and if a student in her vicinity whispered she would say: "Do you not realize you are in the presence of a genius?" Whatever enhances gender equality enhances male domestication. Women are beginning to rally against the tolerance of rape in India. One of the ironies of recent history is the fact that minority tyrannies in the Middle East have sometimes been secular regimes that liberated women. Whatever the benefits that may eventuate from the fall of Saddam Hussein in Iraq, Gaddafi in Libya, and al-Assad in Syria (seemingly inevitable), the advent of populist regimes will not be positive for women.

Middle-Eastern men have become aware of what they face. Virk (2012) says that historically, men have tended to be free spirited, adventurous, and wild. He describes five stages of domestication: courtship—a man wears clothes and uses perfumes agreeable to women and affects an interest in culture; declaration—he must express love rather than compliments to win her; employment—he must get a job (even as a hawker at a bus stop) so she can hold him in esteem; home ownership—she tortures him with an account of how their landlord tried to take sexual liberties and suggests that rather than killing the landlord (the obvious remedy), he buys a home of their own; parenthood—she begins to call him childish names such as "baby" and shifts child care onto him. His complete domestication is signaled when "they go to market with a baby hanger on the husband's back and a patent little handbag in the wife's arm." This description reveals, I fear, a determination to fight in the trenches.

But there is a caveat. As women negotiate as equal partners at home, is not the home retreating? In America, between 1880 and 1970, about 85% of American children lived in two-parent homes; by 2010, this was down to 70% (Aulette, 2010). In fact, the key question is: before 35, how many young men live with a woman today compared to 50 years ago? No one seems to know the answer. There is no doubt that mixed flatting at an early age, particularly at universities, is common. Even men who forever fall into the single category encounter women in their offices as equals and date a wider range of women as casual-interaction females. There is no doubt that equality in all of these relationships is greater than in the authoritarian home. There is also the fact that some unattached males and females live in large cities in areas now dominated by gays. Gay neighborhoods are notoriously nonviolent.

4.2 THE OMNIPRESENT DECLINE OF VIOLENT BEHAVIOR

The two great world wars of the twentieth century and the threat of nuclear war popularize the notion that we are as violent as the people of earlier times. However, two Harvard academics dissented; one because of his comprehensive historical knowledge, the other because of his brilliance as a social scientist and command of many disciplines.

In 1959, Crane Brinton published *A history of Western morals*. This was before the Cuban missile crisis of 1962 had shown that America and Russia could back away from using nuclear weapons against one another (Flynn, 2012).

Despite this, Brinton could not help but notice the decline of institutions based on violence and cruelty. Slavery has existed for thousands of years. Yet, in the nineteenth century, "an overwhelming majority of Westerners came in a few generations to feel that slavery was *wrong*." He points out that certain accepted, even lauded, practices are now thought beyond the pale of civilized conduct and that if they still exist, are either much tamed or only pursued clandestinely. Dueling is gone and today's private warfare, clan feuds, gang wars, and lynching, are nothing compared to a century ago. Prizefights are tame compared to the cruel exhibitions of the past and blood sports (fox hunting and bull fighting) are struggling against extinction. The mentally ill attract sympathy rather than derision or beatings; the sexually unorthodox attract acceptance rather than prison. He is of course still apprehensive about violence between nations (Brinton, 1959, pp. 435–438).

In the eighteenth century, the brutal treatment of criminals was first lamented. The "disgrace" suffered by a family that had a suicide faded. In the nineteenth century, the notion that society should aid rather than ignore or condemn the unfortunate gained ground, and the presumption that officeholders would steal as much as they could was forfeited. In the first half of the twentieth century, aside from the decline of lynching and private warfare, the winning of the West through the slaughter of Indians was becoming less glorified. Slaughtering people on the highways so we could enjoy our drink, the intoxication of speed, or the manly desire to use a car as a tool of combat when challenged were questioned (Brinton, 1959, pp. 324, 325, 364, 365, 387, 391).

I will make a personal interjection here. When I was a child in the 1930s, I cannot recall any audience that did not take unalloyed pleasure in Charlie Chaplin's films. I still see them as works of genius. But watch them and you will notice that anyone with a crutch may have it kicked out from under them and any elderly person is eligible to have his beard pulled, all in good fun. I have a special interest in the politics of the US abolition of slavery. Southern Senators considered it their right to challenge Senators like Thaddeus Stevens to duels. On one occasion, he was caned on the floor of the Senate and permanently crippled (what alternative did they have, given his cowardly refusal to grant satisfaction to men of honor?). It is true that he had a black mistress. So did they; but they had the decency to keep them hidden.

The better angels of our nature (2011) by Steven Pinker, is a masterpiece of modern social science. He promises to use quantified evidence to show that all forms of violence have declined, whether within the family, within the neighborhood, between tribes, or between nation states. The triggers have been "impersonal" factors like technology, trade, effective government, and new ideas. He lists six trends in historical order, that is, from the one that began first to the one most recent.

First, since about 5000 years ago with the development of agriculture, there has been a trend toward living in cities or city states that discouraged the chronic feuds and raids that characterized societies reliant on hunting, gathering, and some horticulture. Cities added to the wealth and the comfort of people by developing the arts, division of labor, trade, and walls and defenses. War between cities led to larger communities swallowing smaller communities.

The relevant measure is not the absolute number of deaths (population was growing) but the risk individuals bore of dying from violence rather than other causes. As for violent death from war: hunter–gatherers (14,000 BC to 1770 BC) get a rate of 15 per 100 deaths. Beginning with the early cities and empires of recorded history, the rate falls to 3–5%. In the modern period, even the most violent centuries are below the lower value. The religious wars of the seventeenth century killed 2% and the wars of the twentieth century about 1%. Even the holocausts of the twentieth century bring its rate to "only" 3%, and there were exterminations difficult to estimate in previous centuries. Perhaps a better measure is the chance the average person has of dying from violence in a given year. The usual metric is violent deaths per 100,000 people. Several nonstate societies have been singled out as nonviolent, the Inuit (Eskimos), the IKung of South Africa, and the Semai of Malaysia. All of them were three times as dangerous as the United States in its most violent decade (the 1970s). America at present shows about 5 people per 100,000 and Western Europe 1 per 100,000. The "far north" of America (New England west to Oregon and Washington) is as safe as Europe but homicides escalate as you go south (Pinker, 2011, pp. 49, 55, 93).

Second, about 1400 AD, at least in Europe, there began a trend away from a multiplicity of feudal territories toward large kingdoms each with a civil authority that could enforce the king's peace and heavily engaged in commerce. Armed conflict between feudal lords was endemic; travel a gamble with death; and booty a major source of income. A king wanted none of this. He wanted a peaceful realm that supplied him with soldiers when needed, and tax revenue based on untroubled peasants and trade, thus increasing the national wealth. Trade was important because it was mutually beneficial. You do not kill a profitable trading partner the way you may another feudal rival to raid his property.

In thirteenth century England, the homicide rate was over 20 per 100,000 per year. From the sixteenth to the twentieth century the rate steadily dropped down to less than one. The fall in other European nations is even more spectacular. In the thirteenth century, many nations were more violent than England (the Italians were the worst at almost 100 homicides per 100,000) but all reached the same low level by the twentieth century. Men were responsible for 92% of the killings, and they murdered mainly in their early 20s before domestication by women (Pinker, 2011, pp. 60–64, 68, 77, 78).

Violence was once more prominent in the upper class (men of honor). In Medieval Europe, it was common to take revenge by cutting off noses. Today, violence is mainly present among the lower class, but even there it is quite low in Europe and the far north of America. It survives where the cult of honor is a lower-class phenomenon, as in the American South and among Black youth. Many Blacks also distrust the civil authorities and therefore, settle disputes among themselves rather than appealing to the law (Pinker, 2011, pp. 81–85). Worse, Black women in America suffer from an unfavorable marriage market. For every 100 Black women of marriageable age, there are only 57 Black males who are viable (alive, not felons, and employed). Thus fewer Black men marry and undergo domestication (Flynn, 2008, chap. 2).

Third, as Brinton pointed out, the seventeenth and eighteenth centuries shift away from cruelty toward humanity. Pinker adds detail. Fewer amusements like roasting a cat alive to entertain the general public and royalty, or men competing to batter a pig to death with clubs. Whipping a boy when a prince was naughty stopped (you could not whip a prince but someone had to be whipped). Public exhibitions of criminals being hung or drawn and quartered, breaking people on the wheel until they were simply a screaming mass of shapeless flesh and splintered bones, keelhauling sailors (dragging them by a rope around the ship's hull until they drowned or were cut to pieces), these things ended.

The last heretic was tortured; the last witch burned in Europe in 1749. The Duke of Brunswick took two Jesuits to see a "witch" being tortured and said, "I suspect these two men of being warlocks." She screamed, "You are quite right." She had seen them turning themselves into goats and wolves, and knew that they had fathered children with heads like toads and legs like spiders. People stopped killing each other for being Catholic or Protestant. People became literate and aware that their customs were their customs and no more natural than those of other peoples (Pinker, 2011, pp. 67, 138, 139, 145–148, 175).

Fourth, between 1946 and today, there is the period of the long peace. Since World War II, no great power has engaged in direct combat with another great power, and developed states in general have stopped fighting one another. This may seem cherry picking given the holocaust during World War II. It was particularly horrible because a "civilized" nation isolated an ethnic group. But if those killed are added to war deaths and then divided by of the world's population, the total for World War II comes out ninth. Those ahead of it include the Lushan Revolt in China (755–763) that killed one-sixth of the world's population (eight times the total for World War II) and the thirteenth century Mongol conquests (five times). I am not sure that the desire to kill anyone at random was in the perpetrator's favor. Genghis Khan: "The greatest joy a man can have ... is to drive (his enemies) before him." Each horseman was assigned a quota of men to be killed and brought back ears as a proof. He concludes his ecstasy: "To see the faces of those dear to them bedewed with tears, and to clasp their wives and daughters in his arms" (Pinker, 2011, pp. 195, 196).

After World War II, great powers fought to retain their colonies but eventually gave up. England and France made a last-ditch effort to coerce Egypt. The United States and the Russians used proxies to fight in the Korean War. They both intervened in the Middle East and sustained or overthrew governments. Nations that were divided had a terrible civil war to achieve unification (Vietnam). Nations that underwent collapse butchered each other (Yugoslavia). But the disgust that European states might fight one another again is palpable. At one time, this was not so. The expectation that great powers would fight one another was normal. All of the following fought at one time or another: The Hapsburgs, Spain, France, England, Russia, Germany, America, Italy, Turkey, Japan, China, and the Netherlands and Sweden, until these last two abandoned great power status (Pinker, 2011, pp. 222, 223).

Fifth and last, between 1989 and today, for almost 25 years, there has been the period of the new peace. Civil wars, genocides, repression by autocratic governments, and terrorist attacks have all declined. To forbid one nation attacking another, the absolute foundation for peace is this commandment: no wars shall be fought to annex territory across present national boundaries (there are a few violations of this, primarily in the Middle East, that we will address later in this chapter). This was pioneered in Africa where the national boundaries left behind by the colonial powers were so fragile that any disturbance threatened universal anarchy. But it has spread to the world in general.

The lesser evil is that some burning injustices are left unresolved, such as the fragmentation of the Kurdish nation. Let us hope that in the distant future these can be settled by negotiation. Since America's intervention in Afghanistan and Iraq, which were not aimed at revising international borders, there has been a reluctance to intervene in Libya and now in Syria (Pinker, 2011, pp. 258–261, 338–340, 350–352).

4.2.1 Violence Turned Inward

It would be less amiable if violence has simply changed its target with less harm to others compensated by more self-harm (such as suicide or self-mutilation). Freud endorsed the thesis that our violent tendencies are fixed and if not directed outward, they will be directed inward. However, the prediction that there will be an inevitable trade-off between the two has often been refuted. Slovenia may have a low murder rate and a high suicide rate, but Italy is low for both. Nonetheless, the data for the past is largely missing (I am going to ignore whether they lacked the "internal tension" we feel today). The rise in suicides throughout much of the West seems entirely due to people living longer: individuals generally wait until old age to kill themselves. The best I can do is draw on Menninger's *Man against himself* (1938) and argue that there are many outstanding examples of self-punishment which are no longer duplicated.

We are impressed by the Jonesville massacre of 1978 when 909 people participated in a suicide cult (another nine were murdered). In 1757, the founder of the Skoptsi sect used a blazing hot iron to mutilate his sexual organs. Quoting scripture he believed that Adam and Eve had sinned by entering into sexual relations. He baptized hundreds and each was enjoined to attain the rank of apostle by recruiting 12 new members. Entire Russian communities were converted. One mass conversion totaled 1700, and the group attained a membership of over 100,000. Many castrated themselves (Menninger, 1938, pp. 221, 222).

Despite insinuations that some members of the Knights of Columbus wear hair shirts, those who attain the fourth degree are warned that common sense must prevail. They may wear capes, swords, and jewels of office, but even pierced jewels are discouraged (they are also warned against unscrupulous vendors of self-punitive devices).

It was not always thus. Saint Marcus of Alexandria carried 88 pounds of iron with him and always slept in a swamp. His follower Saint Eusebius carried 155 pounds of iron and lived in a dry well. Some saints joined the grazers who spent their entire life on all fours on the mountainside and ate grass like cattle. There were those respectful of nonhuman life. Saint Simeon Stylites stood on a pillar for most of his life. He switched to one leg for a year, the other being covered with hideous ulcers. He chastised those who picked worms from his sores, saying, "Eat what God has given you" (Menninger, 1938, pp. 99, 100, 113, 114).

Menninger (1938, pp. 55, 208, 291, 292) does not spare those who indulge in self-mutilation today. They range from people who bite off all their fingernails and start consuming their fingers, commit suicide by hugging red-hot stoves or swallowing suspender buckles, and those who are accident-prone. The champion was someone who fell from his cradle and broke his right arm, drove a hatchet through his left foot, was gored by a bull, fell off a freight train which crushed his left side, drove his car off a 45 ft bank, and finally was caught in the explosion of a gas stove that enveloped him in flames (he was saved). This is only a partial list. The absence of psychoanalysts and newspapers in earlier times leaves us bereft of such accounts from the past.

4.3 COGNITIVE PROGRESS AND MORAL PROGRESS

We know that magical and religious beliefs produced either immoral or counterproductive behavior in the past: the pyramids as wasted effort, human sacrifice to feed the Gods (the Aztecs killed about 1.2 million), the burning of witches, and the horrors of the Inquisition. The person on the rack had a "soul" that would spend endless years in Paradise if only they would convert under torture. Georg W. Oesterdiekhoff (2009) has traced the effects on ethics running from magic to religion to a scientific knowledge of reality.

We know about how faith can destroy reason and humanity. God instructs his chosen people how to slaughter animals. When Aaron's two sons do so using the wrong kind of incense, he burns them alive. God was enraged that the Israelites spared women during their slaughter of the Midianites. They are to complete the genocide, with the incentive of raping nubile sex slaves along the way. Other people starting with the Hittites and ending with the Jebusites are to meet the same fate. When allowed to capture women, the latter may not be in the mood for sex having seen their husbands slain. God advises his children to shave her head, pair her nails, and imprison her until she sees the wisdom of being raped. Saul was jealous of David because women in his court are singing: "Saul has killed by the thousands, but David by the tens of thousands" (Pinker, 2011, pp. 7–9).

Pagan myths anticipated many Christian myths (the flood or the virgin birth or the resurrected god); this was dismissed because Satan had anticipated Christianity to discredit faith. For all the slaughter of Christians in the Roman arena, more Christians killed one another (3000) over who should be bishop of Adrianople than had died in 10 years of the last pagan persecution. Early on, Tertullian extolled holy ignorance: "We have no need of curiosity after Jesus Christ, nor of research after the Gospel."

During the Middle Ages, what day was a time for fasting was more important than fundamentals of right and wrong. Luther's followers put the number of devils at 2,665,866,746,664. After being thrown into deep water, witches were burned if they floated: water was innocent and would reject an evil thing. God's intelligent design proved to be beneficial: He had allotted only 2 eggs per year to the crane (distasteful) but the pheasant and partridge (delicious) laid 15 or 20 per year. Benjamin Franklin's invention of the lightening rod was forbidden because it protected buildings from God's wrath (he used lightening to punish people). Victorian fundamentalists objected to the umbrella. God had said that rain should fall on the just and the unjust (Brinton, 1959, pp. 177, 279; Hallpike, 2008, pp. 285, 358; Smith, 1953, pp. 183, 224, 293, 295, 341).

But are we fully aware of what it was like to live everyday life surrounded by such superstition? In many tribal societies, every natural death was a murder and innumerable innocent people were executed. It is horrible to contemplate that some of them thought that they were guilty: what if they had wished the person dead or had dreamed about their death? When murders occurred, using divination to establish the guilty party was counterproductive, assuming that punishment is meant to deter crime. Many walked free ready to kill again. In Europe, inherited guilt (the Garden of Eden) was common. This was not directed simply at Jews in the vicinity (Christ killers). Crusaders to the Holy Land sometimes believed they were off to punish people who were literally responsible for Christ's death. In Europe, people lived huddled in shacks frightened by priests and terrorized by the devil. The sheer amount of time spent warding off the devil was staggering. Children were beaten to drive the devil out of them. Children were tainted by the illegitimacy of their birth.

The personification of animals was inherited from tribal society. From the thirteenth to the eighteenth centuries, animals thought complicit in murder, assault, plague, or bestiality (sometimes true) were tried and executed throughout Europe. They included pigs, bulls, horses, cows, sheep, rats, beetles, and insects. They were provided with lawyers (usually before church courts) and always heard whatever testimony was brought against them. Some were clearly wronged: in 1474, a rooster was prosecuted for laying an egg fathered by Satan. On the other hand, some were exonerated: lawyers won famous victories representing rats and beetles (Evans, 1987).

In India, trial by elephant prevailed. By the time of British India, the new sciences had made their way among the educated classes, and British colonials condemned what Europe had condoned a century earlier. In nineteenth century America, there was another instance of when civilizations overlapped. In 1840, George Callis rescued American Indians by leading them away from a firestorm. He found those saved were resentful. The horse's hoofs had awakened a fire god so he was responsible for both cause and effect.

By 1900, the new scientific ethos had blind faith on the defensive. However, it did nothing to banish the secular demons of nationalism and militarism. These dominated even the best minds of that time. In 1914, when Wittgenstein volunteered for the Austrian army, one of his acquaintances said with amazement, "He wants to get a gun and run around killing people." Thomas Mann had long felt the need of a war to subordinate materialism to "German *Kultur*." Rilke called the outbreak of the war the resurrection of "the God of hosts." Max Weber gushed "this war is great and *wunderbar*." Even the saintly Martin

Buber, who later opposed the identification of Zionism with Jewish nationalism, lost his mind: "I know personally that Belgian women amused themselves by putting out the eyes of wounded German soldiers and forcing buttons ripped from their uniforms into the empty eye sockets" (Elon, 2003).

4.3.1 Morality Today

In the twentieth century, cognitive progress had more subtle effects on moral progress. Nationalism and racism peaked during World War II. But after that, among those whose minds altered as the century progressed, these idols have been on the defensive. The same is true of cruel moral maxims that treat individuals as if it they deserve to suffer without fault. At this point, massive IQ gains begin to tell a tale of moral as well as cognitive liberation. I do not mean the gains themselves, of course, but the larger significance of the new habits of mind they signal. Let us see if we can illuminate the connection.

Remember that the modern mind broke its ties with the concrete world, the dominant theme as late as 1900, and asked us to take the hypothetical seriously and use logic to analyze abstract concepts. How did these habits of mind take moral reasoning away from the stone age of simply accepting the bias and cruelty of the past?

First, there is taking the hypothetical seriously. In Chapter 1, Luria gave many examples of how people once thought: not deducing that there might be white bears at the North Pole and not deducing that there might be no camels in Germany. When combating racism, taking the hypothetical seriously is the foundation of mature moral argument. In 1955, when Martin Luther King began the Montgomery bus boycott, young men of my acquaintance, home from college at 21, had dialogues with their parents or grandparents. Question: "What if you woke up tomorrow and had turned black?" Reply: "That is the dumbest thing you have ever said, who do you know that turned black overnight?" When Luria's subjects said "How can I solve a problem if it isn't so?" they were serious. They simply were not willing to take the hypothetical seriously.

As for nationalism, my *Beyond patriotism* (2012) diagnoses the retreat from patriotism by some of the American public between World War II and today. Try this question: "What if your home was hit by a drone because someone nearby was sheltering a Taliban?" Or better: "If a war killed so many foreigners to save 3000 Americans, where would you fall off the boat: at 10,000 or 100,000 or one million?" The answer tends to divide the youth from the aged (the latter: "their government protects them and our government protects us"). Voltaire said that all man's reason flies before a drum. Well, it depends on how much reason and how loud the drum.

Second, see Chapter 1 once again, today we use logic to analyze abstract concepts. This is a powerful weapon against local norms that incorporate the cruelty of the past as a residue. Islamic fathers shock the world when they kill a daughter because she has been raped. We would ask: "What if you had been knocked unconscious and sodomized?" He is unmoved. He sees moral maxims as concrete things, no more subject to logic than any other concrete thing like a stone or a tree. He does not see them as universals to be generalized by logic. Today the tendency is to express moral maxims as generalizations and try to make them logically consistent with one another. Question from one of my students: You say we should never judge the customs of another culture; yet you are also an advocate of women's rights. What do you say about the practice of female circumcision? Whatever the conclusion, this is a far cry from primitive moral reasoning.

In other words, these habits of mind did not merely help us to adapt to modernity. They also taught us how to modify the modern world thanks to more mature moral reasoning. They taught us to stride toward freedom with Martin Luther King and take seriously the "collateral damage" of killing foreigners in Vietnam and Iraq and Afghanistan. No general today would talk about "bombing the Vietnamese back to the stone age." I am aware that everyone has not taken the first steps away from racism or nationalism or cruelty, and that many factors have diluted prejudice. However, as someone who has spent his entire life as a scholar and lecturer doing moral philosophy, and began that task in the South in 1957, I know that reason is not insignificant.

I hope that my account of the contribution of reason to morality does not give religion in itself a bad look. It did not invent crusading fervor. Crusading fervor did just as much harm when taken over by the Nazis or Stalinists of the twentieth century. Can we say that the retreat of racism and nationalism has rendered us immune from infection? I think that this is true of Europe. Despite the rise of neo-Nazi parties, they will never get beyond a fringe, as they show when they moderate their policies when office beckons.

The Sunnis and Shiites are still capable of religious slaughter, witness when they fought for control of the streets of Baghdad. But they seem focused on turning violence against one another and the state of Israel rather against the outside world (except when we enrage them by meddling in the Middle East). Note how Pinker charted the decline of terrorism. These people can inflict damage. But if, and I grant that the "if" is not secure, modernization eventually comes to the Middle East, they will lose ground.

4.4 PROGRESS AT RISK

Pinker has reservations about the persistence of progress over the balance of the twenty-first century that any cautious scholar, mindful of the dangers of prophecy, would articulate. I will be bolder about predictions and express alarm. My concern is engendered by the fact that a factor that once pacified humanity is now a powerful barrier to dealing with the most important threat we face: climate change. And by the fact that some actors are still ignoring a rule: the most important rule for maintaining peace.

In the past, the more nations that enjoyed economic progress and engaged in international trade, the better. Today, the momentum of economic progress promises to make the problem of cutting carbon levels in the atmosphere impossible. I have drafted a book on this topic and cannot replicate it here. I will describe the relevant trends.

It is true that the skeptics are correct when they say that there are cycles that affect temperature and have nothing to do with carbon. They are correct when they say that temperatures have been at present levels in preindustrial times, well before we began to escalate emissions. But that does not mean carbon counts for nothing. There has never been a time in the earth's history when the carbon content of the atmosphere has been above 1000 ppm (parts CO_2 per million) and when the polar ice caps still existed. The disappearance of the ice caps would be a disaster. The West Antarctic glacier is looking increasingly fragile. If a large chunk of it goes, the world would experience a sea level rise of 3.3 m (10 ft).

Imagine the earth, some centuries hence, when temperate zones appear only as you approached the Polar Regions. A race is going on between: how much carbon dioxide we emit per unit of economic output, which is diminishing by 1.3% per year; and how fast economic growth escalates, which is about 3.45% per year. We are not even close to winning the race.

Figure 4.1 gives the projections. We pass 500 ppm (which some call the point of no return) by 2050 and the no-polar-ice-caps value of 1000 ppm soon after 2100. To win, the rate of economic growth would have to fall despite the fact we will have 10 billion people, rather than 7 billion, by the end of the century. People in the developed world would have to lower their standard of living. The present trend of raising people in the developing world out of poverty would come to a tragic end. This is why the Kyoto talks go nowhere. What American President is going to accept targets that would have him face reelection on a platform of less prosperity? What Chinese leader is going to tell his rural poor that they are going to stay poor? What is needed is a new vision: how to stop temperature rise without cutting the growth rate that is the only hope of the world's poor.

This means that we must buy time until we develop really clean power. It means accepting climate engineering. If that seems unnatural, how natural is it to pollute the atmosphere with carbon? Stephen Salter of Britain has proposed by far the least dangerous method. At a cost negligible compared to the costs of climate change, a fleet of ships would send sea spray upward to whiten the clouds and reflect away the sun's heat. It is anticipated that they could be controlled in a way that would leave present patterns of

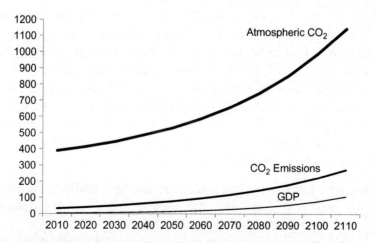

Figure 4.1 Atmospheric CO$_2$ projections from 2010 to 2110.

rainfall undisturbed. This would actually lower the earth's temperatures and in the meantime, we could develop the only really clean power possible: that of using either lazars or plasma to achieve fusion of hydrogen. US Congressmen see no point in this and continually threaten funding cuts.

The odd thing is why anyone right or left or center, even those who deny any role to carbon, would object to arresting temperature rise or developing an energy source that could guarantee economic progress without a darker side. Human survival is not at stake but human progress may be reversed for the first time in 10,000 years. Where is the international intellectual consensus necessary? Perhaps it is easier for cognitive progress to pay moral dividends when habits like generalization and taking the hypothetical seriously have automatic application. Perhaps a new vision is too much to ask of rationality in its present state of development. I hope not but I make no predictions.

The territorial commandment that "no one uses force to annex territory" is fundamental to banning war over the twenty-first century. The Middle East is volatile because of the antagonism between Sunni Muslims and Shiite Muslims, perhaps the last groups that possesses a crusading ideology, at least when one gets behind the leadership to the grass roots. The only nation that attempted to annex territory by force over the past 25 years was Saddam Hussein who attacked Kuwait in 1991.

However, there is an ambiguity that creates a far more dangerous situation. Many regard the 1967 border between Israel and the occupied territories on the West bank of the Jordan as the potential border between Israel and a Palestinian state. Thus, even moderate Arab opinion sees Israeli expansion of settlements in that area as a violation of the territorial commandment. This gives camouflage to extremists who preach a crusade to eliminate Israel. Terrorist groups harass Israel with all means of sabotage they can command. When they get drones, this may reach intolerable levels.

Wars and even a nuclear exchange in the Middle East may not blight the next 100 years. But it is quite possible and the destruction this would engender bodes ill for the Islamic World or the world in general that trades with that area. Climate and regional tensions: we must meet a long list of challenges during the twenty-first century. Whether China or America makes more efficient use of the new eugenics over the next few generations does not loom large.

REFERENCES

Aulette, J. R. (2010). *Changing American families.* London: Pearson.

Brinton, C. (1959). *A history of Western morals.* New York, NY: Harcourt.

Brüne, M. (2007). On human self-domestication, psychiatry, and eugenics. *Philosophy, Ethics, and Humanities in Medicine, 2,* 21. doi:10.1186/1747-5341-2-21.

Elon, A. (2003). *The pity of it all: A portrait of the German–Jewish epoch 1743–1933.* New York, NY: Picador.

Evans, E. P. (1987). *The criminal prosecution and capital punishment of animals.* London: Faber and Faber. (Original work published 1906).

Flynn, J. R. (2000). *How to defend humane ideals: Substitutes for objectivity.* Lincoln, NB: University of Nebraska Press.

Flynn, J. R. (2008). *Where have all the liberals gone? Race, class, and ideals in America.* Cambridge UK: Cambridge University Press.

Flynn, J. R. (2012). *Beyond patriotism: From Truman to Obama.* Exeter, UK: Imprint Academic.

Hallpike, C. R. (2008). *How we got here: From bows and arrows to the space age.* Central Milton Keynes, UK: AuthorHouse.

Leach, H. M. (2003). Human domestication reconsidered. *Current Anthropology, 44,* 349–368.

Mahfouz, N. (1956). *Palacewalk.* New York, NY: Anchor Press. (Trans. 1990: William Maynard Hutchins & Oliver E. Kerry).

Mahfouz, N. (1957a). *Palace of desire.* New York, NY: Anchor Press. (Trans. 1991: William Maynard Hutchins, Lorne M. Kerry, & Oliver E. Kerry).

Mahfouz, N. (1957b). *Sugar street.* New York, NY: Anchor Press. (Trans. 1992: William Maynard Hutchins & Angele Botros Samaah).

Menninger, K. (1938). *Man against himself.* San Diego, CA: Harcourt.

Oesterdiekhoff, G. W. (2009). *Mental growth of humankind in history.* Norderstedt, Germany: Norderstedt Bod.

Pinker, S. (2011). *The better angels of our nature: The decline of violence in history and its causes.* London: Penguin.

Smith, H. (1953). *Man and his gods.* London: Jonathan Cape.

Virk, S. H. (2012). *The domestication theory.* <http://worldpulse.com/node/49936> Accessed 25.02.2012.

Wilson, P. J. (1988). *The domestication of the human species.* New Haven CN: Yale University Press.

CHAPTER 5

Genes and Individual Differences

All of us must be pleased that humanity has enjoyed some cognitive and moral progress over the millennia and over recent generations. However, what about our genes and our own personal life history? To dodge the effects of genes on individuals would be to underestimate their importance. We can have huge IQ gains between generations that are environmentally caused and nonetheless find that genes are potent in determining how an individual compares with another individual within a generation. The fact that genes co-opt powerful environmental factors within a generation does not obviate the fact that it *does* co-opt them. Therefore, genetic differences between individuals are far more predictive, concerning the cognitive abilities of individuals during their own lifetime, than certain environmental differences that separate them. For example, more important than being born into a privileged family rather than a somewhat less privileged one.

Have our genes robbed us of autonomy in terms of our own cognitive development? I fear that what follows will necessitate mastering more technical detail than hitherto. The next 10 pages may prove difficult. But assuming the results are sound, and the results will strike all knowledgeable experts as sound, the reader can still assess whether genes rob individuals of significant choice. If frustrated, you may want to skip to that topic, which begins under the heading "Family and Fate."

5.1 AGING AND FAMILY ENVIRONMENT

The story of an individual's cognitive abilities is really a story of growing up. In early childhood, parents try to treat their children equally despite the fact that they have genetic differences, so they impose a common family environment that is very potent. Indeed, the home environment their own children have in common, distinguishes them from the children of a family more enriched than their own. But as they grow up and enter school and eventually establish a peer group, the home loses its potency to the larger world, which does *not* treat them the same despite their genetic differences. Even within a family, even as a preschooler, one child may take advantage of what parents can offer better than their siblings. Throughout their school career a genetically-favored child gets extra attention, extra books to read, joins a book club, enters an honors stream, makes bookish friends, and so forth. As family environment fades, the quality of genes gets more and more matched to the child's current quality of environment.

At this point, most readers would object that while this makes sense, surely the fact that one is born into an underprivileged family could not fade entirely. It has something to do with what school you attend and what friends you make and should leave some kind of indelible mark throughout life. Setting aside circumstances that are off the normal scale of environments (being shunted from one foster home to another until 18), the evidence shows that our reactions are mistaken. Scholars put the point as follows: say by the age of 17 or 20, the proportion of IQ variance (between individuals) explained by family environment has simply disappeared in favor of variance explained by the matching of genes and one's current environment (for quality). Usually they call family environment "common environment" so as to distinguish between being raised within one family rather than within another.

As stated, when family environment fades, our genes tend to become matched with our "current environment." Nonetheless, current environment can do a great deal to raise or lower an individual's IQ compared to what it would be on a strict hierarchy of genetic endowment. At any age, individuals can have good luck (take a course that challenges them) or bad luck (brain trauma from a traffic accident). These nonfamily aspects of environment are there for everyone. But when people are lumped together into groups, it may not count for much because whatever good happens to this one and whatever bad happens to that one tend to even out.

I will analyze groups that cluster around a certain level of cognitive performance, that is, groups that average at the 98th percentile for vocabulary, groups that average at the 84th percentile, and so forth. These are ideal for assessing at what age family environment fades. But they do conceal the fact that the *individuals* grouped at those levels may have current life experiences that make them atypical, atypical of a group average that implies a match between cognitive level and quality of environment.

5.2 THE NEW METHOD

I am going to use a new method of trying to convince you of these trends. As you know, the accepted method of estimating the contribution of genes and family to IQ variance is the kinship studies. We measure the potency of shared genes by studying identical twins separated at birth. This gives a measure of how individuals with no common family environment are atypically close thanks to identical genes. In addition, we compare the IQs of adopted children to their natural siblings. This gives us a measure of how individuals with no shared genes are atypically close for IQ thanks to being raised in the same home. There are also other kinship studies, such as fraternal twins (no more alike genetically than brothers or sisters) raised in the same home.

There are problems with these designs. Adopted children are rarely tested up though the adult years and adoptive homes do not include poor quality homes. Identical twins still have a common prenatal environment and they may be assigned to homes no different than those of relatives. Trends from one age to another have to be pieced together from many studies. Although the collective evidence shows that the effects of family or common environment fade away by adulthood, the age is uncertain and its influence may differ from one cognitive ability to another. Results do not cover the whole range of ability levels. Above all, kinship studies are expensive and arduous.

The method suggested here costs nothing, takes a few days, and gives results by age and mental ability. It exploits a new source of data: the performance of standardization samples on Wechsler IQ tests. Child samples are from the manuals for the WISC (Wechsler Intelligence Scale for Children) 1947−48, WISC-R 1972, WISC-III 1989, and the WISC-IV 2002. Adult samples are from the WAIS (Wechsler Adult Intelligence Scale) 1953−54, WAIS-R 1978, WAIS-III 1995, and WAIS-IV 2006. The dates refer to when the samples were actually tested. The Wechsler IQ tests have 10 or 11 subtests and one of these is vocabulary.

I will analyze the vocabulary subtest. It deals with words in common usage and not technical terms. It is the most predictive of performance on the other subtests and subsequent life history. The new method can be used on all subtests common to the WISC and WAIS and on any other test that provides similar data from youth to old age.

5.2.1 Detecting the Presence of a Planet

Sometimes we detect the existence of a planet that we cannot see by what it does to other heavenly bodies. If they are pulled out of their natural orbit by gravity, there must be a planet nearby whose gravity does the pulling. I am going to detect the effects of family environment by measuring its influence on other factors. If it exists it should distort a certain "pattern" when we compare children with adults. The pattern assumes continuity from WISC data to WAIS data. Experts may wish to consult the Box that discusses this problem.

Detail About Matching Ages

Those who know about WISC and WAIS samples may need some reassurance. When we compare those 17 and older with their "parents" (people 28 years older), we can stay entirely within the WAIS data. It covers all ages from 17 to old age. When we want to match younger children with their "parents," we have to link WISC and WAIS data. For example, to compare 12-year olds with 40-year olds, there are three steps: norming the 12-year olds on their 17-year-old WISC companions; norming the 40-year olds on their 17-year-old WAIS companions; and then adding the two differences (how much 12 falls short of 17 plus how much 17 falls short of 40).

The WISC 17-year olds and WAIS 17-year olds may not quite match for quality, for example, the 1995 WAIS-III sample might have been a bit substandard (Flynn, 2012a). But this should make no difference because the comparisons with 17-year olds are internal to the WISC and WAIS data sets, respectively. As long as the WISC 17-year olds are comparable to the younger children in the sample, and as long as the WAIS 17-year olds are comparable to the older adults in the sample, the link is sound. I pair children with adults 28 years older because that was the average age of parents at the birth of a child in America between 1950 and 2004 (fathers tend to be 3 years older than mothers). As for pairing the various WISC and WAIS standardizations, the dates are close enough so that we are comparing adults and children at about the same time, namely, from 4 to 6 years apart. I have split the dates in half so that WISC/WAIS is put at 1950.5 and the others at 1975, 1992, and 2004, respectively.

5.2.2 What Does the Planet Do?

Assume that mature adults by say, the age of 40 or 45, have entirely shed the effects of family environment. We will revisit that later. Assume that because we are dealing with group averages, the effects of current environment on individuals within those groups, for better or worse, average out to nil. If that were true, these adults when grouped by performance level would attain a perfect match between genes and current environment. After all, the distortions of family environment and current environment are gone. Therefore, as we saw in Chapter 1, the genetic quality of the adults would attain a near-perfect match between quality of genes and quality of environment.

Now imagine we look at children and we find that the perfect match is missing. We can tell this by norming the children against the adults. If at every level of group performance the pattern is still there, we should observe the following: at the 98th percentile of performance, children should need a certain improvement to match the adults at that level; at the 84th percentile, children should need that same improvement to match the adults; at the median, the children should need that same improvement to match the adults; and so forth down to low percentiles.

But what we find is that the gaps between children and adults vary systematically. At the high levels they are further from adult performance than they are at the lower levels. So we detect the influence of something present among children and not among adults. I will argue that this is primarily family environment. Children at the 98th percentile of performance are being pulled *downward* by family environments that are, on average, below that percentile on the hierarchy of families by quality. Children at the 2nd percentile of performance are being pulled *upward* by family environments that are, on average, above that percentile on the hierarchy of families by quality.

5.2.3 Measuring the Pull of the Planet

Surely the above makes sense. As long as family environment is influential, it can hardly be the case that every child at the 98th percentile of performance is from a family that hovers around the 98th percentile of quality. Their family environments would range from the very top down to perhaps the average environment. Surely every child at the 2nd percentile of performance is not from a family that hovers around that low percentile. Their family environments would range from the very bottom up to perhaps the average environment. In both cases, we see the pull of family environments mismatched with genes, a potency that distorts the adult pattern.

As to how to measure that potency, we can take the score gap between children and adults at the median as our yardstick. Because at the 50th percentile level of performance by children, the number of family environments above or below that percentile would cancel out in terms of quality. The children at the median would, on average, be spread over the full range of family environments. Therefore, they would have the same match of genes and quality of environment we find at the median for adults. All we have to do is calculate the difference between the child/adult scores at the median and the adult/child difference at high levels and we are measuring the negative effects of family environment. As these children are handicapped, they have farther to go to match the adults who are their counterparts and the extra distance gets a plus. When we calculate the difference between the child/adult scores at the median and the adult/child difference at low levels, we are measuring the positive effects of family environment. Since these children benefit, they have less far to go to match adults and the reduced distance gets a minus.

5.2.4 What is the Planet's Name?

There is no real alternative to citing family environment as the main distorting influence but there is an ambiguity. There are three components that affect the variance between the IQs of individuals: genes, family environment (often called common environment), and current environment (often called uncommon environment).

Genes would be only a minor distortion and if anything, would cause a small underestimate of the pull of family environment. The notion that children far above the median for vocabulary should benefit from a greater and greater advantage for genes as they age is not plausible. But there might be a small negative effect. As the handicap they suffer from an unfavorable family environment fades, they might need slightly less elevated genes to attain such a good vocabulary.

As we have seen, current environment has a lot to do with the bad or good luck no one can protect people from. No doubt, those that score high on vocabulary at any age enjoy better luck than the average person. But the question is whether this advantage would rise or fall with age. If so, it would mean something like: high performers have a certain balance in terms of favor of good over bad teachers at 6; high performers would see that balance change for better or worse in terms of fewer or more teenage traumas at 16; and high performers would see it change again in terms of more rather than less unemployment at 26. If this were true, you would expect that twin or kinship studies would show that the percentage (of IQ variance) current environment explains would alter from age to age. In fact, kinship studies show that uncommon environment is steady at about 25% at all ages (Haworth et al., 2010; Jensen, 1998).

5.2.5 The Planet Gradually Disappears

In sum, as they age, children are shedding some negative pull at the top levels of performance and shedding some positive pull at the bottom. The main tug is likely to be the effects of a family environment that is either inferior or superior to their level of performance. When those effects are gone, they attain a perfect match of genes and environment at all levels. And the demise is signaled by an adult/child score gap at all levels that matches the gap at the median. Appendix B gives a more elaborate defense of the method for those unconvinced.

5.3 THE METHOD APPLIED

I will compare children (ages 6−25) to older adults at various performance levels: the median, 1 SD above the median (84th percentile), 2 SDs above the median (97.73 percentile), 1 SD below the median (16th percentile), and 2 SDs below the median (2.27 percentile). All differences between adults and children are equivalent to IQ points (SD = 15).

Table 5.1 presents the child versus adult comparisons at 4 years that represent the midpoint of when the WISC and WAIS were normed: 1950.5, 1975, 1992, and 2004. Look at the average differences between adults and children (in bold). Deviations from the adult/child gap at the median are prominent at higher and lower levels. They run in the expected direction, greater above the median, less below. For example, note the comparison between ages 13−16 and age 42.5. The score gap at the median is about 19 points (SD = 15). But the two values above the median show about 22−24 points, and those below show 13−15 points. At least, that pattern holds up through the age of 17.

To estimate the potency of the mismatches between genes and family or common environment, we must subtract the adult/child gaps at

Table 5.1 Adult Versus Child IQ Differences at Four Times at Five IQ Levels

Adult Age	35	37.5	40	42.5	45	45–55	
Child age	6–8 (−)	8–11 (−)	11–13 (−)	13–16 (−)	17	18–20 (−)	20–25 (−)
+2 SD (1950.5)	66.54	50.69	34.53	21.54	13.37	9.78	7.17
+2 SD (1975)	71.52	52.11	35.70	21.06	11.79	10.73	3.23
+2 SD (1992)	75.81	52.91	38.58	25.49	12.75	9.00	7.50
+2 SD (2004)	67.13	46.29	32.58	20.91	13.13	9.00	7.01
Average	**70.25**	**50.50**	**35.35**	**22.25**	**12.76**	**9.63**	**6.23**
+1 SD (1950.5)	62.36	49.68	36.60	23.60	15.65	8.81	5.18
+1 SD (1975)	70.07	47.88	32.55	21.44	12.50	9.99	2.13
+1 SD (1992)	78.50	50.49	36.72	25.70	17.25	11.34	11.34
+1 SD (2004)	67.50	48.86	34.70	24.24	18.29	16.01	12.00
Average	**69.61**	**49.23**	**35.14**	**23.75**	**15.92**	**11.54**	**7.67**
Median (1950.5)	55.88	37.87	25.88	15.27	9.53	4.07	0.81
Median (1975)	65.91	43.05	29.06	20.54	13.40	9.11	2.67
Median (1992)	−	47.36	30.69	20.91	15.84	14.25	14.25
Median (2004)	−	40.23	28.34	19.13	12.00	11.25	8.25
Average	**−**	**42.13**	**28.49**	**18.96**	**12.69**	**9.67**	**6.50**
−1 SD (1950.5)	−	−	18.68	10.49	7.01	1.95	1.95
−1 SD (1975)	−	−	22.19	14.06	9.17	8.33	−0.41
−1 SD (1992)	−	−	27.02	18.26	11.88	10.62	10.62
−1 SD (2004)	−	−	25.44	17.45	8.57	7.14	4.26
Average	**−**	**−**	**23.33**	**15.06**	**9.17**	**7.01**	**4.11**
−2 SD (1950.5)	−	−	17.31	7.49	2.82	1.77	1.77
−2 SD (1975)	−	−	17.67	10.92	4.74	3.95	0.00
−2 SD (1992)	−	−	30.09	16.94	8.22	7.85	4.28
−2 SD (2004)	−	−	24.38	16.26	7.50	6.26	3.75
Average	**−**	**−**	**22.36**	**12.90**	**5.82**	**4.96**	**2.45**

the median from those above and below. Above the median, this will normally give a plus and below the median a minus.

Table 5.2 is derived from Table 5.1. Just as we detect the existence of an unseen planet by measuring its gravitational pull, the plus signs above the median and the minus signs below show family environment at work! At ages 11–13 and 13–16, it is a potent force at all vocabulary levels. By age 17, family environment is absent at the +2 SD vocabulary level but influential at all others. By ages 18–20 and ages 20–25, it has faded for all those above the median but is still active below.

Table 5.2 Adult Versus Child Vocabulary Gaps: How Much Do Gaps at Levels Above/Below Median Differ from those at Median?
Child Ages 11–13; Adults Ages 39–41
35.35 (+2 SD) − 28.49 (median) = +6.86
35.14 (+1 SD) − 28.49 (median) = +6.65
28.49 (median) − 28.49 (median) = −
23.33 (−1 SD) − 28.49 (median) = −5.16
22.36 (−2 SD) − 28.49 (median) = −6.13
Child Ages 13–16; Adults Ages 41–44
22.25 (+2 SD) − 18.96 (median) = +3.29
23.75 (+1 SD) − 18.96 (median) = +4.79
18.96 (median) − 18.96 (median) = −
15.06 (−1 SD) − 18.96 (median) = −3.90
12.90 (−2 SD) − 18.96 (median) = −6.06
Child Age 17; Adult Age 45
12.76 (+2 SD) − 12.69 (median) = +0.07
15.92 (+1 SD) − 12.69 (median) = +3.23
12.69 (median) − 12.69 (median) = −
9.17 (−1 SD) − 12.69 (median) = −3.52
5.82 (−2 SD) − 12.69 (median) = −6.87
Child Ages 18–20; Adult Ages 45–55
9.63 (+2 SD) − 9.67 (median) = −0.04
11.54 (+1 SD) − 9.67 (median) = +1.87
9.67 (median) − 9.67 (median) = −
7.01 (−1 SD) − 9.67 (median) = −2.66
4.96 (−2 SD) − 9.67 (median) = −4.71
Child Ages 20–25; Adult Ages 45–55
6.23 (+2 SD) − 6.50 (median) = −0.27
7.67 (+1 SD) − 6.50 (median) = +1.17
6.50 (median) − 6.50 (median) = −
4.11 (−1 SD) − 6.50 (median) = −2.39
2.45 (−2 SD) − 6.50 (median) = −4.05

5.3.1 Corrections

The potency of family environment revealed in Table 5.2 is an underestimate. Take those at +1 SD (the 84th percentile) for vocabulary. Although most will be in families whose quality is below that level, there will be a significant number above. Therefore, the estimates are the differences between two opposing tugs: larger tugs downward by less favorable family environment and lesser tugs upward by more favorable family environment. Take the estimates at -1 SD (the 16th percentile). The estimates are the differences between larger tugs upward and lesser tugs downward. At age 17 at the 84th percentile, there is a downward tug 3.23 points greater than the upward tug. Therefore, we do not know the potency of family environment when it is not at war with itself.

However, we can make assumptions unlikely to be too generous. The calculations are detailed in Appendix B but here I can make evident their plausibility. At the 97.73 percentile for vocabulary (2 SDs above the median), very few of the children would enjoy family environments above that level (the top 2%) and many would be in families below that level (those whose environmental ranking would range from the 97th percentile down to at least the 50th percentile). So the main tug of family environment on vocabulary performance would be downward and only a slight tug would be upward. I have allowed an unfavorable ratio of 51 to 1 as a minimal assumption and 24.2 to 1 as a more plausible assumption. These raise the values in Table 5.2 only slightly. For example, look at the top value on the far right. It applies to children 2 SDs above the median aged $11-13$. In the table, it shows that negative family environments cost them 6.86 IQ points. This now rises to 7.13 points at a minimum and to 7.45 points as more plausible.

At the 84th percentile for vocabulary (1 SD above the median), the adjustment is more liberal. Now a substantial number of the children would have family environments above that level, although far more of them would, of course, still be in the unfavorable environments below that level. I have allowed an unfavorable ratio of 6.75 to 1 as a minimal assumption and 4.07 to 1 as a more plausible assumption. As for the effects, look at the next to top value on the far right. It applies to children 1 SD above the median aged $11-13$. In the table, it shows that negative family environments cost them 6.65 IQ points. This now rises to 8.96 points at a minimum and to 10.98 points as more plausible.

All adjustments at the 16th (1 SD below the median) and 2.27 percentiles (2 SDs below the median) are the mirror image of those at the corresponding levels above the median. At the median itself, I have averaged the two estimates that surround it, that is, the estimates for $+1$ SD and -1 SD.

5.4 DECLINE OF FAMILY ENVIRONMENT

Finally, we can cash in the significance of all of this. We can trace how much the impact of family or common environment declines with age. Table 5.3 is derived from Table 5.2. It includes the unadjusted values for how much family affects IQ differences between these groups of individuals [CE(1)], the conservative adjustments [CE(2)], and the more liberal adjustments [CE(3)]. As noted in the Appendix, these can be translated into the language of scholars. What is the correlation between family environment and the vocabulary performance of children? What percentage of IQ variance between individuals is explained by family environment?

As Table 5.3 shows, the variance explained by family environment drops with age at all vocabulary levels. At +2 SDs, even the more liberal estimate shows the effects are small at ages 11−13 and negligible thereafter. The tiny minus values at ages 18−20 and 20−25 are not logically impossible. If valid, they indicate that those with elite vocabularies have on average actually accessed common environments slightly above their level on the genetic hierarchy. At +1 SD, variance explained is still significant at age 17 and negligible thereafter. At the median, it is significant at 17, but then falls rapidly with age and the effects are small thereafter. At −1 SD, the same is true except the variances explained at ages 18−20 and 20−25 have some significance. At −2 SDs, the percentage of variance explained hovers around 5% from ages 11−17 and becomes negligible thereafter.

In Table 5.3, the values at the median are in bold because they would dominate any kinship study. They cover almost 90% of the curve (those who cluster around vocabulary levels +2 SD and −2 SD are the top and bottom 5.45%). The variance explained by family environment fades: 29−43% at age 12, to 15−23% at age 14.5, to 9−14% at age 17, to 4−6% at age 19, and to 3−4% at age 22.5.

It is time to redeem my promise to discuss the assumption on which these estimates are based: that mature adults (ages 40−50) show no effects of family or common environment uncorrelated with genes. The data cannot prove that this is the case and if there were a residue, it would have to be added to all estimates. However, note how precipitously the family share of IQ variance drops with age, indeed it halves

Table 5.3 Decline of Family or Common Environment Effects with Age

Voc. (SDs)	Voc. (pts.)	Points due to CE(1)	Points due to CE(2)	Points due to CE(3)	Cor. (2)	Var. % (2)	Cor. (3)	Var. % (3)	Child ages
+2 SD	+30	+6.86	+7.13	+7.45	0.238	5.66	0.248	6.16	11−13
+2 SD	+30	+3.29	+3.42	+3.57	0.114	1.30	0.119	1.42	13−16
+2 SD	+30	+0.07	−	−	−	−	−	−	17
+2 SD	+30	−0.40	−	−	−	−	−	−	18−20
+2 SD	+30	−0.27	−	−	−	−	−	−	20−25
+1 SD	+15	+6.65	+8.96	10.98	0.597	35.67	0.732	53.59	11−13
+1 SD	+15	+4.79	+6.45	7.90	0.430	18.50	0.527	27.77	13−16
+1 SD	+15	+3.23	+4.35	5.33	0.290	8.42	0.355	12.61	17
+1 SD	+15	+1.87	+2.52	3.09	0.168	2.82	0.206	4.24	18−20
+1 SD	+15	+1.17	+1.58	1.93	0.105	1.10	0.129	1.66	20−25
Median	−	−	−	−	0.530	28.59	0.649	42.92	11−13
Median	−	−	−	−	0.412	15.38	0.505	23.09	13−16
Median	−	−	−	−	0.304	9.21	0.372	13.80	17
Median	−	−	−	−	0.204	4.27	0.250	6.41	18−20
Median	−	−	−	−	0.186	2.86	0.228	4.29	20−25
−1 SD	−15	−5.16	−6.95	−8.51	0.464	21.51	0.568	32.24	11−13
−1 SD	−15	−3.90	−5.26	−6.44	0.350	12.26	0.429	18.40	13−16
−1 SD	−15	−3.52	−4.74	−5.81	0.316	9.99	0.387	14.99	17
−1 SD	−15	−2.66	−3.58	−4.39	0.239	5.71	0.293	8.57	18−20
−1 SD	−15	−2.39	−3.22	−3.94	0.215	4.62	0.263	6.91	20−25
−2 SD	−30	−6.13	−6.38	−6.66	0.213	4.51	0.222	4.93	11−13
−2 SD	−30	−6.06	−6.30	−6.58	0.210	4.41	0.219	4.81	13−16
−2 SD	−30	−6.87	−7.14	−7.46	0.238	5.67	0.249	6.19	17
−2 SD	−30	−4.71	−4.90	−5.12	0.163	2.66	0.171	2.92	18−20
−2 SD	−30	−4.05	−4.21	−4.40	0.140	1.97	0.147	2.69	20−25

from one age to another: from 29−43% (at age 12), to 15−23% (age 14.5), to 9−14% (age 17), to 4−6% (age 19), and to 3−4% (age 22.5). The halving makes it look as if it were trending to zero. Certainly, the momentum of the decline would go on after age 25. If there really were a residue in the early 20s, the trend would eliminate the last vestige of family environment within a few more years.

It may seem odd that family environment counts for no more at −2 SDs, that is, where vocabulary performance is far down on the scale, and that this holds true no matter what the age. Does this not imply that

Turkheimer, Haley, Waldron, d'Onofrio, and Gottesman (2003) were mistaken when they found that environment was more influential at low levels of socio-economic status (SES) than at higher levels?

There are no implications for SES whatsoever. Our hierarchy is a hierarchy for richness of vocabulary. It is sad that those with genes for vocabulary at the cutting line for mental retardation (−2 SDs) have a close match between their genes and quality of environment. From an early age, others react to them as mentally retarded and treat them as such. It is no surprise that those at elite levels for genes match environments that are almost equally enriched. They appear brilliant and are treated as such.

5.4.1 Family and Fate
Before we dismiss the effects of family or common environment on life history, it is worth taking into account that it still differentiates individuals at the age of 17. I emphasize this because that is the age at which Americans take the SAT (scholastic aptitude test) to qualify for university entrance. The same age of testing holds throughout much of the world.

At 2 SDs above the median for vocabulary, there is no mismatch between competence and environment inclusive of family environment. Therefore, the "typical" person at that level has no "family deficit" to take into account. However, at 1 SD above the median, we find that an average mismatch costs 3.23 points. Therefore, those who score at that level are at the equivalent of 115 IQ points of vocabulary performance when a perfect match between competence and family quality would put them at 118.23.

I will translate this difference into what it entails for scores on the SAT-Reading. De la Jara (2012) of Mensa has equated IQ and SAT scores. His table equates (allowing for the passage of time) with my calculations made some two decades ago (Flynn, 1991). The typical family deficit at +1 SD translates into an SAT-Reading score of 543 rather than 567 (the SAT SD is 110 compared to an IQ SD of 15). In Table 5.4, I provide a list of 20 universities whose SAT-Reading score cutting lines make them relevant. Universities will not tell their minimum score, but there is data for the score that isolates the bottom 25% of their students (Grove, 2012). Note that a score of 567 would have made you viable or near viable at universities ranging from UCLA to the University of Connecticut. While your actual score of 543 forbids these and means you border on nonviability at universities ranging from Minnesota to the University of Vermont.

The price of the typical family deficit is actually worse than this. By using the unadjusted value for family environment, I have merged those few who profited from a positive mismatch between competence and environment with the many who suffer from a negative mismatch. For every favored person, there are more than four handicapped. And their price is probably not just 24 points on the SAT-Reading but something like 40 points. If my results were to extend to the SAT-Writing and the SAT-Quantitative, the total SAT score deficit would be 72–120 points, which every American parent will recognize as something that often separates joy from tears. It is very likely that vocabulary level strongly influences performance on the writing test. As to the quantitative, we need a similar analysis for the Wechsler sub-test that measures arithmetical reasoning.

Table 5.4 then offers a similar scenario for the influence of family deficit on the part of those at the median. In fact, there cannot be an average mismatch between competence and environment because for every person handicapped there is someone favored. But as this implies, there is a lot of family deficit at work, so I have used an esti-mate that is the average of those 1 SD above and 1 SD below the median. As Table 5.4 shows, for this group, their SAT score of 415 is 25 points below the no family deficit score of 440. They have missed out on the cutting line for viability at universities ranging from Michigan State to Southern Connecticut.

Those at 1 SD below the median typically benefit. On average they enjoy environments above what a match with their competence would dictate. Therefore, I have defined a family deficit as follows: merely having a perfect match between competence and environment rather than having the typical beneficial family environment. Recall that there would be only one handicapped person for every four favored people. But also recall that their bad luck would be a few points greater than the table shows. You might think that those at the 16th percentile for vocabulary would have no chance for tertiary education but there are plenty of open entry colleges, junior colleges, and community colleges. I did find a few universities whose cutting lines for the bottom 25% of their students made them relevant. A typ-ical SAT score of 325 gives you a few of these to shoot at, but a

Genes and Individual Differences

Table 5.4 Disadvantaged Family Environment and College or Life Prospects (Age 17)					
	Vocabulary Scores			SAT-Reading Scores	
	Perfect Match of Genes and CE	Average Mismatch of Genes and CE	Disadvantaged IQ Points (SD = 15)	Perfect Match of Genes and CE	Average Mismatch of Genes and CE
+1 SD	118.23	**115.00**	3.23	567	**543**
	25th percentile SAT-Reading at selected universities				
	Brigham Young (Utah)	570	U. Denver	550	
	Pittsburg (Pennsylvania)	570	**Score of 543**		
	UCLA (California)	570	Ohio State	540	
	U. Florida	570	U. California San Diego	540	
	Score of 567		U. Delaware	540	
	Baylor (Texas)	560	U. Maryland (Baltimore)	540	
	Beloit (Wisconsin)	560	U. Minnesota	540	
	U. Georgia	560	U. Texas (Austin)	540	
	Clemson (South Carolina)	550	U. Texas (Dallas)	540	
	Florida State	550	U. Vermont	540	
	U. Connecticut	550	Virginia Tech	540	
Median	100.00	100.00	(3.38)	440	**(415)**
	25th percentile SAT-Reading at selected universities				
	Score of 440		Western Kentucky	430	
	Corcoran Art & Design	440	Colorado State Pueblo	420	
	Louisiana Tech	440	Hawaii Pacific	420	
	Michigan State	440	Southern Arkansas	420	
	U. Nevada-Las Vegas	440	Southern Connecticut	420	

(Continued)

Table 5.4 (Continued)				
	U. South Alabama	435	U. Hawaii Hilo	420	
	Adams State (Colorado)	430	U. North Alabama	420	
	Eastern Kentucky	430	U. Wisc. (Whitewater)	420	
	Fairleigh Dickson (NJ)	430	**Score of 415**		
	Colorado Mesa	430	Arkansas State	410	
	Kansas Wesleyan	430	Arkansas Tech	410	
−1 SD	**81.48**	85.00	3.52	**299**	325
	25th percentile SAT-Reading at selected universities				
	Dakota Wesleyan	340	**Score of 325**		
	Oklahoma Panhandle	340	Tougaloo (Mississippi)	320	
	Upper Iowa	340	**Score of 299**		
	Presentation College (SD)	330	Faulkner (Alabama)	281	
−2 SD	**63.13**	70.00	6.87	–	–
	A vocabulary score below 70 forbids even basic functional literacy				

perfect match score of 299 put virtually every university out of reach (except open entry).

At 2 SDs below the median, an IQ of 70, the penalty for a merely perfect match score is not what university you attend but whether you attain even basic functional literacy. For those with a merely perfect match, we see a vocabulary IQ of 70 reduced to 63.13, but recall that somewhere between 24 and 51 people are favored for every person with a perfect match. Given that those who cluster around 2 SDs below the median are 5.45% of the population, and that at least 5% of Americans lack even basic functional literacy, whatever environment they have at present needs to be enhanced by better special education.

Although I have singled out the age of 17 as one at which typical family deficit or being worse than typical has important life consequences, its influence at lower ages should not be discounted. It is a disadvantage at ages like 12 and 14 not to have the vocabulary to profit from your school subjects. Someone who does not enjoy serious literature at that age may never develop the habit of reading that literature for enjoyment. Granted that by mature adulthood, all will be made good in the sense that you will enjoy a vocabulary environment that matches your place on the genetic hierarchy for vocabulary. This blessed state may not compensate you in human terms for a family deficit that dates from your youth. It may have had some lasting effect on your self-esteem, who you married at university, what your children will aspire to, and your general quality of life.

Creating a perfect match between genes and environment is not some transcendent ideal. The highest goal is to eliminate the worst environments, encourage those who seem to be falling short of their potential, upgrade everyone else's environment as much as we can, and each live life to the full.

5.5 MAKING YOUR OWN LUCK

What about you as an individual? If you are an adult, the influence of family environment has faded. But the cognitive environment you live in today, even though it has no persistent effects that correlate with your upbringing, is still a potent influence. Is that such a bad thing? After all, rewriting history is never a choice, so you cannot alter what family you were born into. But you can choose to manipulate the current environment that conditions your mind.

Recall the percent of IQ variance that I have referred to as good and bad luck: throughout life this amounts to 25%. Environment does not stop conditioning your mind. After you turn 21, things still happen. You are drafted and subjected to military discipline, your children or an enervating divorce or illness deprive you of peace of mind or the energy to think, you lose your cognitively demanding job and sink into the despondency of the unemployed. All of these examples seem to imply that you are the mercy of chance.

However, you can make you own luck. A feature of the cognitive environment that has a powerful impact on a person is the internal environment he or she carries around in his or her head. Just as an average athlete may adopt a training schedule more demanding than average, and carries it with him to be followed wherever he goes, so you can fall in love with ideas and create an internal gymnasium that exercises your mind from day to day. It was said of my old professor Leo Strauss that he never seemed to think of anything but political philosophy from the moment he awoke until he closed his eyes at night. For sanity's sake, this is not advised. But you can exercise your mind by reading great literature and history, thinking about the wonders of evolution and cosmology, equipping yourself with the basic tools you need to understand the modern world, such as elementary economic analysis, an image of good science and social science, a propensity to use logic to criticize whatever moral or political argument you may hear or use (Flynn, 2010, 2012b, 2012c).

This gives you a gymnasium of the mind that is not only internal but also portable. You can still read in the army and think what you like at least within limits (to the military mind, independence of thought is a kind of treason). Just as the vicissitudes of failed human relationships and unemployment cannot immobilize a runner who doggedly continues training, they lose potency when confronted by a lively mind.

If people maximize internal cognitive environment, would that show up in our own data? Only if it behaved like family environment and disrupted the pattern. It would have to favor some level of performance more than others and vary by age. For example, assume that elite vocabulary performers collectively created a positive internal cognitive environment more effectively than those at all other levels. This makes sense: the most gifted in terms of vocabulary might well tend to create an internal world that was more cognitively challenging. But they would also have to compare favorably with elite adults. Those aged 18−25 have to be better at this than those aged 40−50. And they would have to do it after the deleterious effects of family environment faded. Otherwise their advantage would be lost when swamped by the negative pull of family at that level. Recall my comments on Table 5.3. It shows tiny minus values at ages 18−25. At the time, I said that these might show that the phenomenon described was registering.

The fact that the phenomenon is unlikely to be visible in our data does not show that it has no effects. If tomorrow everyone upgraded his internal cognitive environment, it would be like an IQ gain over time: there would be far superior cognitive performance overall compared to what we have at present. At present, some are undoubtedly doing the upgrading while others are not. And everyone who does it asserts her autonomy.

Genes do set limits on individual achievement. No doubt, they also set limits on the progress of humanity over time, whether cognitive or moral and the latter includes some limit on the nonviolent behavior of human beings. But nothing can destroy your autonomy to fall in love with the good and live a better life than your proclivity toward violence might dictate. Nothing can destroy your autonomy to fall in love with ideas and cognize at a level superior to any that your genes might seem to dictate at present.

5.5.1 Aspirations

Before abandoning the individual, there is good news about what you may aspire to as an occupation. This is true no matter whether you have upgraded your internal environment and enhanced your cognitive abilities, or whether you are content with the IQ your genes and ordinary environment dictate.

In 1980, Jensen (p. 113) set 110 as the average IQ of high school graduates with the warning that the average graduate has only a 50/50 chance of graduating from university. He set 120 as the average IQ of college graduates. Only some of the latter would have been accepted for higher degrees and he puts the average for a Ph.D. at 130. This would put the average for those accepted for a higher degree at about 125. He has no hesitation citing data collected in 1960. These IQ estimates are still with us. I get emails from colleagues in New Zealand and overseas expressing shock that someone is doing graduate work with an IQ of 115.

These IQ thresholds simply show that in 1960, only those well up the IQ scale received an education that conferred credentials and opportunities. Since then, mass education at the tertiary level has demonstrated that those with much lower IQs can meet its demands and the demands of cognitively demanding jobs. Look back to Table 5.4 and you will find that the average person (with an IQ of 100) is viable at many universities ranging from Louisiana Tech to Michigan State to Farleigh Dickson. They have SAT scores that put them above the lower 25% of those in the first year class.

No university flunks as many as that, although some drop out because of financial problems, lack of motivation, or ill health.

Therefore, an IQ of 100 means you can graduate from a good university and even those below that will survive if they work hard. Let us say that the IQ threshold for graduates is 95. Using the table of values under a normal curve, if you take the top of the curve from 95 on up, the mean IQ would be 109 for university graduates. Assuming universities are as selective today as in the past, the mean for those doing higher degrees would be about 114. Thus, the person considered suspect when doing a higher degree was actually mildly superior at an IQ of 115.

To get a mean for those doing higher degrees at 114, the minimum threshold for acceptance would be an IQ of 103 (eliminating all those under 100, only boosts the average to 112). So do not be intimidated by obsolete tables and what your guidance counselor tells you. Average Americans can aspire to professional and subprofessional posts without feeling daunted. After all, 35% of them hold those posts at present.

5.6 IQ GAINS VINDICATED

What IQ thresholds fettered Americans in the past? If the mean for graduate study was 125, the threshold had to be 117.6. This tells us something of supreme significance about the reality of IQ gains over time. Over 50 years, between 1960 and 2010, the threshold for acceptance for higher degrees fell from 117.6 to 103 or a difference of 14.6 IQ points. What were the IQ gains over that period? WAIS gains were 16 points from 1953—54 to 2006 (Table 2.5). Reduce those 52.5 years to 50 years and you get 15.2 IQ points.

The two are almost identical. IQ gains over time reduced the threshold for those qualifying for elite jobs by almost 15 points. This shows that the gains paid off in the real world of occupational performance. Doctors and managers and bankers and lecturers and technicians can spot the people who did those jobs 50 years ago 15 IQ points and still do the jobs. There is one possible rebuttal: the jobs are less cognitively demanding today. My medical colleagues tell me that doctors have to know more science today, my commerce colleagues tell me managers have to plan with a wider range of knowledge, and my economics colleagues tell me that merchant bankers today are virtuosos of cognitive complexity. University academics today sometimes give coherent lectures and do research; university technicians are infinitely more knowledgeable than in the past.

Of all the evidence brought forward, the falling thresholds are the best evidence that the cognitive progress of the last century is real rather than an illusion.

REFERENCES

de la Jara, R. (2012). How to estimate your IQ based on your GRE or SAT scores. Google "IQ comparison site".

Flynn, J. R. (1991). *Asian Americans: Achievement beyond IQ*. Hillsdale, NJ: Erlbaum.

Flynn, J. R. (2010). *The torchlight list: Around the world in 200 books*. Wellington, New Zealand: AWA Press.

Flynn, J. R. (2012a). *Are we getting smarter: Rising IQ in the twenty-first century*. Cambridge UK: Cambridge University Press.

Flynn, J. R. (2012b). *Fate and philosophy: A journey through life's great questions*. Wellington, New Zealand: AWA Press.

Flynn, J. R. (2012c). *How to improve your mind: Twenty keys to unlock the modern world*. London: Wiley-Blackwell.

Grove, A. (2012). College admissions. About.com.guide (search by each state).

Hawworth, C. M., Wright, M. J., Luciano, M., Martin, N. G., de Geus, E. J., van Beijsterveldt, C. E., et al. (2010). The heritability of general cognitive ability increases linearly from childhood to young adulthood. *Molecular Psychiatry, 15*, 1112–1120.

Jensen, A. R. (1980). *Bias in mental testing*. London: Methuen.

Jensen, A. R. (1998). *The g factor: The science of mental ability*. New York: Praeger.

Turkheimer, E., Haley, A., Waldron, M., d'Onofrio, B., & Gottesman, I. I. (2003). Socioeconomic status modifies heritability of IQ in young children. *Psychological Science, 14*, 623–628.

APPENDIX B (PRIMARILY FOR SPECIALISTS)

I will try to make good on the promises this chapter makes, one by one.

Defense of the Method

Whatever the method measures, disappears at about ages 17–25. This is in accord with the disappearance of the effects of family environment on IQ variance as measured by the kinship studies, at least when dealing with the population as a whole. Because the kinship studies show that only family or common environment disappears by then, with uncommon environment marching steadily on, the implication seemed to be that I am measuring family environment alone. But I was puzzled.

After all, I was using a method that registered how much environment was pulling vocabulary scores up or how much environment was pulling vocabulary scores down. Could not something other than "bad" family environment (below the 98th percentile) or "good" family environment (above the 2nd percentile) be at work?

This meant a closer examination of uncommon environment, which I have described as the good or bad luck our current environment may hold for us at any age. It is not simply luck of course. Being incapacitated by a freak accident is luck, but as I say in the text, you can make your own "luck" by manipulating your current environment to your advantage and your cognitive ability affects your capacity to do so.

Assume you are of high ability and that as you mature and become more autonomous, you do more and more to create events that are favorable. You evade the draft (for principled reasons I hope), avoid driving recklessly, and create more of an enriched internal environment. If you do these things more effectively as you age, it means that your immaturity "forfeited" an environmental advantage when you were young that was realized as you progressed to adulthood. Therefore, when measuring the extent to which a high-performing person was handicapped by environmental disadvantage before maturity, my method was measuring both "poor" family environment and the youthful "lack of creating fortuitous events" factor. You can construct a similar scenario for low-performance people. Eventually they make their own "luck" but do so badly: get drafted, drive recklessly, create an impoverished internal environment, while at earlier ages they are protected by social institutions that limit their pernicious autonomy, such as school, no car to drive, and so forth.

The method also assumes that by the age of 40 (the standard against which all else is measured) the pattern is set: family environment is gone; and the differences between what autonomy reaps from one ability level to another are constant. The latter means that by 40, what benefits high ability creates over the deficits low ability creates are constant by age, at least between people 2 SDs above the median, 1 SD above the median, the median, 1 SD below the median, and 2 SDs below the median. By then, maturity has established the differences between levels that growing autonomy entails. As always, as far as individuals are concerned, real bad or good luck is still at work but this evens out when you compare whole groups by ability.

Therefore, I must concede that my method may be contaminated. In childhood, it may measure both bad/good family environment and worse/

better events that have to do with lack of autonomy (power to create favorable/unfavorable events). But nonetheless, whatever I measure, the total package does seem to disappear simultaneously with the effects of family environment, so the method is a good measure of the precise age of the demise of the latter. And it does so with better sampling, less cost, by ability level (ranging from far above to far below the median), and by subtest (in terms of each cognitive ability rather than just global IQ).

A few answers to critics that have weighed in: first, the kinship studies really do show that family environment fades away by maturity, at least for the general population as a whole; second, the distinction between family or common environment and uncommon environment is not hard and fast. My being dropped on my head differentiates individuals within the family in that my brother has not been dropped. But being dropped on your head may be more frequent in low-IQ homes than in high-IQ homes, so at that point it shows up as a between-family difference. All I can say is that my method would catch the "drop" event insofar as it differentiates families. But as long as the possibility of contamination is present, my method cannot exclude a "drop" factor emanating from nonfamily differences.

Finally, here is a challenge to those who reject the method in its entirety. If the method is spurious, you should offer a hypothesis that explains the following: why do its results tally so beautifully with the results of the kinship studies? What exactly is at work that produces such a coincidence? Using 40-year olds as a base, *something* disappears from IQ variance that penalizes high achievers and benefits low achievers; something that has declining influence from infancy to maturity. What is it?

Correction to the Potency of Family Environment

When commenting on Table 5.2, I argue that the estimates of the potency of family environment contained therein are an underestimate and promise a more detailed treatment in this Appendix. Here, we shall derive the actual values used to make the corrections. Table 5.3 is based on Table 5.2. It gives values for correlations between family environment and vocabulary IQ, as well as the percentage of variance family environment explains. These estimates will also be made explicit.

Recall that the estimates in Table 5.2 are the differences between two opposing tugs. Above the median, the plus estimates are the result of large tugs downward from worse family environments and lesser tugs upward from better family environments. The plus values represent, of course, an overall handicap that increases the score gains needed to match adults. Below the median, the minus estimates are similar. They are differences between larger tugs upward and lesser tugs downward, and represent an overall benefit that cuts the score gains needed to match adults. How can we estimate the potency of family or common environment when it is not at war with itself? I will try to make assumptions unlikely to be too generous.

At the 97.73 percentile for vocabulary, I will assume: the children are spread over common environments from the top of the curve down to the median as if the curve were neatly sliced at the median. There would be too few above 4 SD (one-tenth of 1%) to give special weight, so all those in the top 2.27% get an advantage that ranges from 0 to 1 SD (put it at 0.5 SD). The product of these two is $+1.135$. Then 13.73% $(16 - 2.27)$ suffer from an environmental deficit that ranges from 0 to 1 SD (0.5). The product is -6.865. Finally, 34% $(50 - 16)$ suffer from a deficit from 1 SD to 2 SDs (1.5), which gives -51.00. The sum of these is 57.865.

The ratio of better to worse is 1.135 to 57.865 or an unfavorable ratio of 51 to 1. The adjustment then follows automatically. Take the 6.86 points from Table 5.2 (children 11–13 at $+2$ SDs): $51x - 1x = 6.86$ (52); $50x = 356.72$; $x = 7.13$ points as the true potency of common environment at the $+2$ SD level. This is its potency to resist regression to the mean. So we can calculate a correlation coefficient for the $+2$ SD level (30 points above the mean): $7.13/30 = 0.238$. Squaring the correlation gives the percentage of variance explained: $0.238 \times 0.238 = 5.66$.

This is a conservative adjustment. It is not just that it gives a ratio of 51 to 1 in favor of the downward pull over the upward. It is the assumption that this elite group is so heavily represented in the area from the median up to 1 SD above the median. This puts 34 environments out of 50 at this level and they are given triple weight (1.5:0.5). A more liberal assumption would be that the curve of environments is tailing off at this point to no more than in the area immediately above (the 13.73 in the area of 1 SD above the median to 2 SDs). This gives a new product for the lowest area: $13.73 \times 1.5 = 20.595$.

Now we get a ratio of better to worse of 1.135 to 27.46 (20.595 + 6.865) or an unfavorable ratio of 24.2 to 1. This more liberal adjustment generates: $24.2x - 1x = 6.86$ (25.2); $23.2x = 172.872$; $x = 7.45$ points. That divided by $30 =$ a correlation of 0.248 and when squared, 6.16 as percentage of variance explained. Note that the conservative and more liberal assumptions do not make a great deal of difference.

At the 84th percentile, I assume: the children are spread over common environments from 3 SD above the median (the 99.865 percentile) down to 1 SD below the median (the 16th percentile) as if the curve was neatly sliced at those two points. So 2.135% (99.855 − 97.730) get an advantage that ranges from 1 SD to 2 SDs (1.5). The product of these two is +3.2025. Then 13.73% (16 − 2.27) get an advantage that ranges from 0 to 1 SD (0.5). The product is +6.865. The sum of the two is 10.0675. The 34% (50 − 16) immediately above the median environment have a deficit from 0 to 1 SD (0.5), which gives −17.00. The 34% below the median environment suffer from a deficit from 1 SD to 2 SDs (1.5), which gives −51.00. The sum of the two is 68.

The ratio of better to worse is 10.0675 to 68 or an unfavorable ratio of 6.7544 to 1. Take the 6.65 points from Table 5.2 (children 11−13 at +1 SD): $6.7544x - 1x = 6.65$ (7.7544); $5.7544x = 51.57$; $x = 8.96$ points as the potency of common environment at the +1 SD level. This is its potency to resist regression to the mean at the +1 SD level (15 points above the mean): $8.96/15 = 0.597$ (correlation). Squaring gives the percentage of variance explained: $0.597 \times 0.597 = 35.67$.

For a more liberal estimate, assume those in the environments in the area just below the mean are not 34 (out of a total of almost 84) but tail off to 16, meaning a symmetrical distribution of environments above and below the 65th percentile. This gives a new product for the lowest area: $16 \times 1.5 = 24$. Now we get a ratio of better to worse of 10.0675 to 41 or an unfavorable ratio of 4.07 to 1. The liberal adjustment generates: $4.07x - 1x = 6.65$ (5.07); $3.07x = 33.72$; $x = 10.98$ points. That divided by $15 =$ a correlation of 0.732 and when squared, 53.59 as percentage of variance explained.

All adjustments at the 16th and 2.27 percentiles are the mirror image of those at the corresponding levels above the median. At the median itself, I have averaged the two estimates that surround it, that is, the estimates for +1 SD and −1 SD.

CHAPTER 6

Frozen Minds

In 1831, for the first time, a tenor named Gilbert-Louis Duprez hit high C will a full chest voice rather than a falsetto (Hallpike, 2008). Human genes had set no barrier to this achievement for perhaps 100,000 years. But it took a musical tradition begun in 1400, with the advent of multiple voices singing choral polyphonic music, to realize the genetic potential. Soon someone is going to run a marathon in 2 hours. I am in a position to comprehend how amazing this is. At 20, I was a useful varsity runner and could run 3 miles at close to a 5 min mile pace. Running more than 26 miles at a 4 min 35 s pace is simply unbelievable.

It is not surprising that the twentieth century saw an extraordinary enhancement of our cognitive abilities over a few generations. No doubt, our genes set limits on human progress, but history shows that no one has any real notion where those limits lie.

However, after the discovery of genes and the fact that genes took thousands of years to alter substantially, the stage was set to ignore history. There developed a steel chain of ideas that put cognitive abilities into a deep freeze as far as enhancement was concerned. According to the twin or kinship studies, the rank order of individuals for IQ and vocabulary shows an almost perfect match between genes and achievement. And the environmental differences between individuals for family background had virtual zero potency by maturity. This left only random environmental shocks to alter that match, such as the good and back luck life holds for all of us. We now had a syllogism: genes are virtually static from one generation to another; systematic environmental counts for virtually nothing; therefore, any evidence of enhancement of cognitive abilities from one generation to another must be largely illusory.

There could, of course, be minor gains or losses due to the effect of increased outbreeding on genes, dysgenic reproductive trends, the effects of nutrition, or less brain damage during delivery. But any gains beyond an IQ point or two must be hollow, for example, due to greater test sophistication. The concept of levels of intelligence that were genetically determined was taken to set strict limits on how much more education could do for those who were not at the top. Thresholds were calculated showing that the mass of people could never aspire to become a technician, much less a professional.

All of this was an illusion. The Dickens/Flynn model showed that a snapshot of the role of genes and the "feebleness" of environment at a given time misses the dynamic interaction of genes and environment over time. We called this the social multiplier. When there is a new stimulus to achievement, the rising mean performance itself engenders new heights of achievement. We used a trivial example to illustrate the point. The advent of TV and the glamorization of basketball set in motion a reciprocal causality that lifted performance to a degree that seemed impossible. People began to make slam dunks, pass the ball with either hand, shoot the ball with either hand, and manipulate their bodies in midair with incredible grace. But the point was important. How genes and environment behave over time is quite different from how they rank human beings in a hierarchy at a given time.

Our model did not, of course, deny the potency of the individual multiplier. When competing with others at a given time and place, who has the superior genes is important. But genes never glue you to a set place on the hierarchy of cognitive achievement. My genes forbade me to set a world record. They did not forbid me to out-train and beat many more talented competitors. My genes forbid me to duplicate the achievements of truly great minds (and a fair swag of people in a class below them). They did not forbid me to fall in love with problems that have exercised my mind and given me an enriched cognitive environment.

Models are complex. It is much easier to refute the thesis of the "genetically frozen mind" conceptually. At a given time the potential of our genetic inheritance is exploited only to the degree that the culture of that time allows. How could this possibly determine what the mind is capable of in radically new social circumstances? How could a static fact, that the vocabulary hierarchy at a given time was influenced by individual differences in genetic endowment, tell us the potential of a dynamic factor, tell us what doubling the years of formal education would do to lift the whole hierarchy to a new level? Unless, of course, we somehow just knew the limits human genes set on the human intellect. But that is sheer assumption: we will know what human genes are capable of only when the best efforts of history run into a stubborn refusal to progress.

I am not saying that those who believed in the frozen mind were obtuse or biased. What they believed was so plausible. When you are immersed in your own time, radical change always seems implausible. Let us take America at the beginning of the twentieth century.

In 1900, professionals were 3% of the population. By 1920, they were still only 5%. They were held in awe because of their cognitive achievements. Even in 1957, when I went to Eastern Kentucky to lecture, I was referred to reverentially as a "PhD man." Who could imagine that by the year 2010, 15% of Americans would be highly paid professionals and another 20% subprofessionals, that is, lower management or technical staff (Carrie, 2012)? If the 17 points of active vocabulary adult Americans gained in the second half of the twentieth century, thanks to the tertiary education revolution, is projected back to 1900, before the secondary school revolution, they made a total gain of 34 points. This is 2.27 standard deviations and puts them at the 98th percentile at that time. Who would have thought that the average person with an average education could replicate the speech typical of professionals in 1900? Who could anticipate that the revered IQ thresholds for various levels of education and occupation would simply be overwhelmed by the weight of numbers?

All of this happened without any upgrading of genes for cognitive ability. As my readers know, I make no claim that the average person today is as "intelligent" as the elite of 1900 (Flynn, 2012). The concept of intelligence carries too much baggage to be useful. I claim only that their minds were not frozen in the mold of that time. They adapted to the modern world and thereby proved far more educable than anyone dreamed. The cognitive history of the twentieth century is the history of the realization of the untapped potential of humanity's genes.

Two groups had elite biases not easy to forgive: those at the top of the cognitive hierarchy were certain that ordinary people would never rival their attainments; those at the top of the social hierarchy were sure that commoners could never play the social roles the aristocrats dominated. Many of the elite championed universal education but I cannot find one who thought that the masses were collectively capable of demanding social roles. They could be made into better citizens and do what they did somewhat better with the occasional genius emerging from the ranks. But that was it.

The arrogance of the "upper classes" comes as no surprise. During World War I, Lord Curzon observed British soldiers bathing: "How is it that I have never been informed that the lower orders have such white skins?" (Blythe, 1964). A pity the lower orders were useful as servants. Otherwise these strange white-skinned creatures could have been kept in zoos. During the intervention in Russia in 1918, General Graves of Britain informed General Groves of America that he was getting a reputation as a friend of the poor and that "you should know that these people are nothing but swine" (Melton, 2001). The lower classes are scum, rabble, riff-raff, louts, peasants, and imbecile yokels sucking on straws.

More surprising, many intellectuals greeted the spread of education with a ferocious pessimism, described by John Carey in *The intellectuals and the masses* (1992). Virginia Woolf and E. M. Forster both devoted themselves to adult education. Yet, Woolf refers to the self-taught workingman as someone "we all knew" to be egotistic, insistent, raw, striking, and ultimately nauseating. Forster has no sympathy with a clerk whose attempts to educate himself are "hopeless." He is simply inferior to most rich people, less intelligent, healthy, and loveable, typical of urbanized rural laborers, who should be stripped of their education and revert to what they can do well: breed yeomen. D. H. Lawrence, Pound, Yates, H. G. Wells, George Bernard Shaw, T. S. Eliot, Aldous Huxley, Evelyn Waugh, and Graham Green also derided the character and capacities of the masses. At times, Carey does not distinguish between portrayal of a character and an indictment of the group to which the character belongs. But he finds some interesting commonalities among intellectuals. The preference of ordinary people for tinned food is considered damning.

Both the aristocrats and the intellectuals were forbidding the tide to come in. Reason has been on the march for a long time and the twentieth century was no exception. Reason is a wonderful thing. When it reaches a certain level it can exploit its new potential with great effect, without the need to progress to a higher level. It does this by sharpening tools (say mathematical notation), automatically invading new areas (moral reasoning), and enlarging vision, for example, showing us how to recognize new problems and solve them through cooperative behavior.

Once human beings learned to reason mathematically, they made enormous advances just by simplifying mathematical notation. Greek symbols for numbers were so cumbersome that it took the genius of Archimedes to represent large numbers. Calculations were so difficult that Aristotle counted it as proof of the rationality of human beings that they could do simple arithmetic. Although Roman numerals were an advance, contemplate the task of dividing MMMDCIX by MCCCIV. As for Algebra, by the time of Descartes, exponents were used and the equal sign was replacing "is equal to." Pity the way Egyptians had to do Algebra using prose: "There is that which added to itself and then again and then again, and then separated into three equal parts, leaves itself with one more thing and one thing still to be divided into three equal parts; what is it?" (The answer is 4: $16/3 = 5 + 1/3$).

The advantage of Leibnitz over Newton was his notation for the calculus. The advantage of Feynman over Schwinger was his notation for quantum mechanics. Cassels and Flynn (1996) not only solved problems to do with curves of genus two and above but also paved the way for others by simplifying the notation.

During the twentieth century, people in advanced societies improved the "notation'" they used to state moral principles. They freed themselves from treating morality as a concrete thing. When they developed the habit of using logic on abstractions and taking the hypothetical seriously, their new habits of mind automatically affected moral reasoning. The bonus was unanticipated but welcome. The Islamic father who kills his daughter for being raped will have a son or a grandson who is accustomed to using logic on abstract principles, rather than treating moral rules as a given. His offspring will be less able to accept logical contradictions in their criteria of justice. Those who restrict entry into the circle of moral concern to a race or nationality will become habituated to using the hypothetical. When raising their own children, they will say "what if your sister did that to you?" They will then have to say to themselves "what if I were black, or an Iranian, or suffered collateral damage through no fault of my own?"

In other words, the continuous taming of our aggressive drives by domestication found a powerful ally in the cognitive revolution of the twentieth century. Those less inclined to seek advantage or revenge through violence find it easier to accept humane moral principles. Those who have humane moral principles find it easier to act on them if they have pacific inclinations and self-control. Better character and better moral reasoning reinforce one another.

The present century presents challenges that could derail human progress. It might seem that we will meet them easily. Dealing with climate change does not require acting on humane principles: enlightened self-interest should be enough. It does not require an end to altruism: the growth that lifts the third world can persist. It merely requires the application of reason to a situation rendered intractable by political realities and economic trends that cannot be altered. Fortunately, there are steps compatible with those realities and trends that hold every prospect of a solution. All that is required is vision: one that puts Salter's ships on the water and funds the quest to get clean energy from laser or plasma fusion. These should be ideas whose time has come.

But history shows that the intrinsic rationality of a vision is not enough. There must be a general consensus in its favor among those whose lives are devoted to thought and speaking and writing and communicating across national boundaries, what Pinker calls the "Republic of Letters." The abolition of slavery was an idea whose time had come only because virtually every leading thinker throughout the world agreed that it was indefensible. The abolition of drift about climate change requires a similar consensus. But where are most of the world's intellectuals? Ignoring the issue because it does not fall within their specialty, and leaving a few specialists to contend with those who see only a conspiracy to deny Americans their guns.

The spread of weapons of mass destruction among nation states and their privatization (falling into the hands of terrorist groups) poses a threat. The norm that guarantees peace, thou shalt not take advantage of power to annex territory, is still fragile, particularly in the Middle East. Israeli intellectuals have reached no consensus as to whether settlements on the West bank violate that norm. Needless to say, intellectuals in Islamic nations must do all they can to dispel the myths that feed fanaticism (such as holocaust denial) and to hasten the spread of modernity. They can fight to replace traditional with modern education, primitive moral reasoning with moral maturity, and enhance the status of women.

Whether human beings can meet the challenges to human progress hangs in the balance. Three commandments should be easier than ten: honor the environment, do not abandon the aspirations of the wretched of the earth, and do not covet thy neighbor's land. To fail entails an almost perverse refusal to pause, take time to reflect, and act. Some wisdom, resolution, and self-control and we might surprise our selves with a better world. One thing is certain: we cannot blame our genes. Nothing about them dictates stupidity in the face of danger. Dysgenic mating is a sideshow.

Whatever happens to us, we can take satisfaction in how far we have come. Living our lives day by day, we take modernity for granted. The very existence of the modern world is astonishing. I refer not to the internet or the air travel or the organ transplants but to the people. No totalitarian regime created a "new man" but without fanfare impersonal social forces have begun the task. The upper classes were so confident that the masses could never match their intellectual attainments and social responsibilities. They were wrong. As Kipling put it, "For the Colonel's lady and Judy O'Grady are sisters under their skins."

REFERENCES

Blythe, D. (1964). *The age of illusion*. Boston, MA: Houghton Mifflin.

Carey, J. (1992). *The intellectuals and the masse: Pride and prejudice among the literary intelligentsia, 1880–1939*. London: Faber.

Carrie, A. (2012). *Occupation change: 1920–2010. Weldon Cooper Center for Public Service*. <http://statchatva.org/2012/04/06/occupation-change-1920-2010/> Note: The 1900 census did not use the same system of classification. However, Carrie put 1920 at 5% professionals and 1910 was 4%. Durand, E. D., & Harris, W. J. (1999). *Population 1910: Occupational statistics (United States Bureau of the Census)*. New York, NY: Norman Ross (Table 14). Therefore, I put 1900 at 3%.

Cassels, J. W. S., & Flynn, E. V. (1996). *Prolegomena to a middlebrowarithmetic of curves of genus 2*. Cambridge UK: Cambridge University Press. (London Mathematical Society Lecture Notes Series 230).

Flynn, J. R. (2012). *Are we getting smarter: Rising IQ in the twenty-first century*. Cambridge UK: Cambridge University Press.

Hallpike, C. R. (2008). *How we got here: From bows and arrows to the space age*. Central Milton Keynes, UK: AuthorHouse.

Melton, C. K. W. (2001). *Between war and peace: Woodrow Wilson and the American expeditionary force in Siberia, 1918–1921*. Macon, GA: Mercer University Press.

Lightning Source UK Ltd.
Milton Keynes UK
UKOW03f1003271213

223637UK00012B/302/P